TWILIGHT
OF THE GODS

TWILIGHT OF THE GODS

Polytheism in the Hebrew Bible

David Penchansky

WESTMINSTER
JOHN KNOX PRESS
LOUISVILLE · KENTUCKY

Scripture quotations from the New Revised Standard Version of the Bible are copyright © 1989 by the Division of Christian Education of the National Council of the Churches of Christ in the U.S.A. and are used by permission.

Scripture quotations from the Revised Standard Version of the Bible are copyright © 1946, 1952, 1971, and 1973 by the Division of Christian Education of the National Council of the Churches of Christ in the U.S.A. and are used by permission.

Book design by Sharon Adams
Cover design by Eric Handel, LMNOP
Cover art (clockwise from top left): (1) Head of a statue of Ishtar, wearing a headdress, from the Temple of Ushtar at Mari, Syrian, 2800–2300 BC (alabaster), Assyrian School / National Museum, Damascus, Syria, Giraudon; / Bridgeman Art Library (2) Mother Goddess Plaque Pendant, from Tell-Ajjul, Israel, 16th century BC (gold), / Ashmolean Museum, University of Oxford, UK,; / Bridgeman Art Library (3) Pendant depicting Astarte, goddess of fertility (gold), Phoenician, (14th century BC) / Louvre, Paris, France, Giraudon; / Bridgeman Art Library (4) Anthropomorphic vase depicting a woman breastfeeding, possibly the goddess Isis, Egyptian (painted red ware pottery) / Ashmolean Museum, University of Oxford, UK,; / Bridgeman Art Library

First edition
Published by Westminster John Knox Press
Louisville, Kentucky

This book is printed on acid-free paper that meets the American National Standards Institute Z39.48 standard. ♾

PRINTED IN THE UNITED STATES OF AMERICA

05 06 07 08 09 10 11 12 13 14 — 10 9 8 7 6 5 4 3 2 1

Library of Congress Cataloging-in-Publication Data is on file at the Library of Congress, Washington, D.C.

ISBN 0-664-22885-2

This book is dedicated to my parents,
Charles and Mimi Penchansky.

Contents

Introduction

Many texts in the Hebrew Bible assume a polytheistic universe. Much of ancient Israelite literature reflects beliefs far more varied than strict monotheism, the belief that only one God exists and all other gods are delusional. From the time of Genesis ("Let us make humankind in our image, according to our likeness") to the Christian tradition's Holy Trinity, notions of monotheism among the people of the book have been less than strict, and always a bit troubled.

Polytheism, in many and varying forms, seems to revisit ancient Israelite texts as a kind of Freudian "return of the repressed." Freud claimed that those parts of our psyche we repress come out in a hidden or dreamlike manner. Certain emotional conflicts, if we force them down, return disguised. Although Israel officially believed in only one God, polytheistic texts come back in the Hebrew Bible like undigested lumps in the monotheistic soup. Notice the following examples:

> Who is like you, O LORD, among the gods [Hebrew, *ʾĕlōhîm*]? / Who is like you, majestic in holiness? (Exod. 15:11)

> You shall have no other gods before me. (Exod. 20:3)

> When the Most High [*ʿelyôn*] apportioned the nations, / when he divided humankind, / he fixed the boundaries of the peoples / according to the number of the gods [*bĕnê Yiśrāʾēl*; "God's children," "God's

sons," or "divine beings"] / the LORD's own portion was his people, / Jacob his allotted share. (Deut. 32:8–9)[1]

For the LORD is a great God [ʾel], / and a great King above all gods [ʾelōhîm]. (Ps. 95:3)

Some of these writers regard other divine beings as colleagues of Yahweh. In each nation, a different national god lived in the land, looked after the people's interests, and received their worship. Yahweh, then, was Israel's god. Other biblical texts write of these gods as rivals for the affection of the Israelites. Some texts regard these other beings as Yahweh's inferiors, his assistants or servants. References to the divine council describe the *bĕnê ʾelōhîm* in this way. In contrast, the three great monotheistic religions each has its own affirmations about the unity and singularity of God. Jews proclaim,

Hear, O Israel: The LORD is our God, the LORD alone. (Deut. 6:4)

In Christianity, the faithful recite the Nicene Creed in many Christian churches:

We believe in one God, the Father Almighty, maker of heaven and earth.

And Muslims declare,

There is no God but Allah, and Muhammad is his messenger.

But the Bible indicates that the ancient Israelites believed differing and conflicting things about God. First, some Israelites believed that only one God existed from the beginning of time. Second, some Israelites believed that only one God existed but that earlier times saw many gods involved in people's lives. Finally, some Israelites (along with most of West Semitic culture) believed that the gods were organized in tiers, and Yahweh inhabited the highest tier alone.[2]

---

1. This is found in the Septuagint version of the Old Testament (*aggelōn theo*) and some of the other ancient manuscripts. The Masoretic Text reads *bĕnê Yiśrāʾēl* ("the sons of Israel," or "Israelites").

2. There are certain variations on this last alternative:

Yahweh inhabited the top tier with a consort, a mother-father god combination.

Yahweh inhabited the second tier as one of the children of the great father god El, or Elyon, whom Yahweh subsequently deposed. Yahweh inhabited the second tier, but usurped the other second-tier gods, and declared himself chief god, El being an absent father (John Day 1998, 172; M. S. Smith 2001, 55).

The second and third of these options would not meet contemporary criteria for monotheism, and yet they too shaped the meaning of monotheism for subsequent generations. In their own way, they each elevate Yahweh above other deities.

Patrick D. Miller suggests that in ancient Israel strict monotheism prevailed over the other theisms: "The understanding and practice of Yahwism that won out over the long run was adamant on this issue of the sole worship of Yahweh, who was without consort or pantheon" (Miller 1987, 240). Upon casual observation that seems to be the case, but a closer look prompts some questions: What does Miller mean by "won out"? Did monotheism win out because of the inherent superiority of its ideas? Did it win out due to divine support and intervention for its position? Did it win out because that is the way the Persian authorities wanted Israelite religion to turn out?[3] Does the fact that monotheism "won out" mean that we must read the entire Bible through this single monotheistic lens?

I want to define monotheism more broadly. I want to include in my definition of monotheism those Israelites who worshiped Yahweh exclusively while acknowledging the existence of other gods. This position is commonly called henotheism. Those Israelites centered Yahweh in their devotion, regarding him as the chief and most powerful god, as the god who specifically cared about their nation. Bernhard Lang calls this theism of early Israel a "qualified monotheism" (Lang 1999, 901). Larry Hurtado, supporting this broader definition of monotheism, has observed, "It is clear that ancient Jews often envisioned a host of heavenly beings, including powerful figures likened to God and closely associated with God" (Hurtado 1998, 7).[4] He wrote this in reference to Greco-Roman Jewish culture, but it can apply in all periods of Israelite history.

Our understanding of Israel and our understanding of monotheism must change. Regarding Israel, we must reconsider the historical narrative that explains how Israel moved from paganism/polytheism to radical monotheism. In this book I mean to demonstrate that many different theisms coexisted within the same society. We are incorrect if we fully link Israel with radical monotheist ideology, as if that were the purest expression of

3. Berquist regards the Persian period as a time when scribes, working for Persian colonial masters and influenced by them, shaped a pan-Israelite sensibility through their production of what came to be the Hebrew Bible (2000, 8–10).

4. He goes on to note, "Graeco-Roman Jews seem to have been quite ready to accommodate various divine beings. . . . Part of the problem in estimating what Jews made of heavenly beings other than God 'ontologically' is that scholars tend to employ distinctions and assumptions formed by Christian theological/philosophical tradition" (21).

Israelite belief. We must acknowledge that there are varieties of monotheisms. Radical monotheism does not exhaustively define and determine the tradition. If, then, we do not allow radical monotheism to be the only way to understand God, how can we define the word "god"?

What is a god? What word might be used to describe how ancient people regarded the notion of deity? Multiple deities? Gendered deities? The inadequacy of the terms used for various types of theism should be obvious when we see contemporary writers groping for subtle distinctions. They either add an adjective to the word "monotheism" (such as "unequivocal monotheism," "pure monotheism," "radical monotheism"), or they coin new terms or phrases ("monolatry," "provisional monolatry," "henotheism"). My personal favorite is from Morton Smith (1971, 29), who describes monotheistic believers as "the Yahweh alone party."[5]

Monotheism might be described most simply as the belief in one god. But such a definition does not preclude the belief in the *existence* of other gods. "You shall have no other gods before me" (Exod. 20:3) By "before me," the writer affirms that other gods actually exist, and might theoretically be brought into Yahweh's presence.

Historically, biblical scholarship has tended to see these two ideologies chronologically, with paganism displaced over time by monotheism. However, the struggle was more an ongoing process, with back-and-forth movement. The ancient Israelites had never quite resolved the "god question," so they oscillated from one extreme position to another.

Therefore, upon the surface of strict monotheism that is the Hebrew Bible, one occasionally sees faint stirrings of another worldview: a world where although Yahweh is the supreme God, he is not always the only god. The literature of the Hebrew Bible gives significant evidence that the Israelites drew deeply from the well of mythology that they found among the people in whose land they dwelt.

I concern myself in this book with a few examples where the Israelite monotheistic consensus breaks down. Does the Hebrew Bible (or at least certain parts of it) allow for divine forces other than Yahweh?

5. See also Lang 1986, 116–25.

Part 1

The Gods of Ancient Israel

Strictly speaking, these five chapters are not *all* about gods. *Miqreh* (chapter 2) is not a divine personality, but more like a force. The Israelites carefully distinguished *miqreh* from the realm of the gods. But the others, Chemosh and the members of the divine council, all fit into the category "gods." They exist as part of the Israelite pantheon, which includes Yahweh. With Chemosh and *miqreh* (chapters 1 and 2) they compete with Yahweh. The divine council (chapters 3 and 4) submits to Yahweh and does his will, but its members are gods nonetheless. Finally, in chapter 5, Second Isaiah satirizes the gods, because he believes they do not exist.

Chapter 1

The Wrath of Chemosh

When Yahweh Lost a War

Mesha's Offering: "A Firstborn We Shall Sacrifice"

Mesha, his back to the wall, performed the desperate act that managed to save his community. Clearly, it was not the first thing that the king of Moab tried, but rather the last. Having seen the blood-red pools picking up the sunlight in the Israelite camp, he attacked, hoping to find the conquering armies in disarray, fighting each other. He was driven back by the intact alliance, the pools being only water in a trick of the sun. Then when his capital city fell under siege, he broke through with a troop of soldiers at what he felt was the weakest point in the line, and was again driven back. And now the Israelite alliance was squeezing his city; both water and food were running low. There was ample precedent for what he was about to do. A Canaanite manual of war written four centuries earlier stated it this way:

> If an enemy force attacks your [city] gates,
> An aggressor, your walls;
> You shall lift up your eyes to Baal [and pray]:
> "O Baal:
> Drive away the [enemy] force from our gates,
> The aggressor from our walls.
> . . . A firstborn, Baal, we shall sacrifice,
> A child we shall fulfill [as votive pledge]."[1]

---

1. There is some question whether this prayer actually refers to human sacrifice at all (Burns 1990, 188).

... Then shall Baal hearken to your prayers,
He shall drive the [enemy/force] from your gates,
The aggressor from your walls.[2]

(Margalit 1986, 62)

If there was ever a time for such a dramatic gesture, this was it. Mesha
ascended the walls of the city and offered his son as a sacrifice to the
Moabite god Chemosh.

How might we regard Mesha's desperate sacrifice? Other biblical texts
portray fathers doing similar things. In stark terms, the writer reports that
Asa caused the "passing [of] his children through the fire" (2 Kgs. 16:3),
but there is no indication of a military crisis to provoke him. The author
of Kings regards child sacrifice as the epitome of evil. In another biblical
account, Lot was willing to give up his daughters to protect his guests, but
no religious sacrifice was intended. The stories of Asa's and Lot's attempts
to dispose of their children indicate that those who offer their children as
sacrifice are contemptible.

More problematic is the example of Jephthah. He too offered his child
to Yahweh, although in his case, the sacrifice occurs *after* the battle. In this
instance (similar to the Mesha incident), the sacrifice is meant to affect the
course of the conflict. Jephthah promises that if Yahweh gives him victory,
he will offer the first one he sees when he returns to his home. From this
story we learn that one can love one's child even when sacrificing her, but
even so, we still feel the horror at Jephthah's action, and the contempt for
his moral weakness remains.

A comparison of Mesha's sacrifice to Abraham's offering of Isaac, however, reveals the following. Each father is ready to offer his heir as a sacrifice to his god. The narrator states that Yahweh never really intended to
receive such a grisly sacrifice, but was only testing the limits of Abraham's
devotion. But there is no doubt that Abraham was ready and willing to do
the deed. Contrariwise, we know that Mesha completed the sacrifice.
Although Abraham traveled to a place of complete privacy to accomplish
his slaughter, the king of Moab slaughtered his son in a public place, on
the walls of his city. The king of Moab carried out his sacrifice, while Abraham did not. However, this was not for lack of intention on the part of
Abraham.

---

2. Margalit, following this translation, goes on to assert, "This text can be dated to about
1250–1200 BC, some four centuries before Mesha of Moab, but the practices it describes are
documented as late as the Roman period." He goes on to give other historical examples.

Perhaps we may thereby judge the two gods, Yahweh and Chemosh, by their relative willingness to drink human blood. Chemosh drinks the blood of the crown prince. Out of gratefulness for this great gift, he will send the Israelites home in defeat and confusion. Yahweh, on the other hand, sends an angel, which stops Abraham's hand just before he brings the knife across his son's throat. Although Yahweh's taste for blood never abates entirely, in this case he chooses not to take a boy's life. In other passages, the slavering God is alive and well. When provoked, Yahweh destroyed the entire earth with a flood, saving a single family, and had to remind himself not to do it again by placing a rainbow in the sky (Gen. 6–9); once Moses had to hold Yahweh back from destroying all Israel because of their slights and rejection (Exod. 32:10). To my mind, Mesha's greater bloodthirstiness makes the portrayal of Yahweh in Genesis 22 less chilling than that of Chemosh in 2 Kings 3. As a result of Mesha's sacrifice, "great wrath" came upon the Israelites and they fled.

For many years I have wondered at such biblical passages that portray Yahweh in heavy competition, as one who meets stiff opposition in the divine arena. This passage, 2 Kings 3, portrays Yahweh as first winning, and then losing in a pitched battle with Chemosh, god of Moab. An Israelite victory is regarded as Yahweh's victory. What do we make of the phrase "great wrath" (*qeṣep-gādôl*)?[3] How we understand the activity of the two gods depends on our interpretation of that phrase.

How might we understand "wrath" in a passage such as this? Most interpretations fall under one of three categories:

1. This narrative represents an older and more primitive notion of Yahweh, which sees Yahweh in competition with the other gods. Later, a purer and more radical monotheism replaced it.
2. This narrative portrays only the power of Yahweh. It does not posit the existence of the Moabite god Chemosh in any way.
3. One may interpret this narrative without recourse to the supernatural.

Montgomery, writing about this phrase in the International Critical Commentary, says regarding other gods in the Bible, "The primitive

---

3. "Ancient interpreters (LXX, Josephus) went to great lengths to avoid the implication that a power hostile to Yahweh was victorious here, but the text is certainly open to that possibility!" (Nelson 1987, 168). Nelson goes on to say, "The nature of the great wrath that saved the day for Moab is left open for readers to interpret on their own" (169).

implication was early ignored and forgotten" (1950, 363–64).[4] He does not address the issue again. He dismisses too easily the possibility that a god, Chemosh, expressed his wrath against the Israelites. Montgomery deems this belief "primitive" because it allows for the possibility of competing gods. He thus assumes what he has set out to prove. He regards the idea of Chemosh's wrath as unthinkable because it contradicts his theology. He assumes that the narrator would never permit such a story into his work.[5] Long describes this process: "How powerful, widespread, and persistent has been the covert impulse to remove ideological embarrassment when faced with a text which can challenge dominant voices of exclusivist monotheism. In effect, these readers refuse the ambiguity that the biblical narrative obstinately permits" (1997, 226–27). Israel, by this view, evolved from belief in many gods, to belief in only one, moving from offering fearful and desperate sacrifices to frightening deities, to obeying Torah in order to please a singular and unique moral God.

Some suggest that the text might have said "the great wrath of *Chemosh*" and that a later editor, uncomfortable with the primitive implication, elided the name.[6] The anger remains as a trace, inscribed by its absence in the text as a remnant from an earlier time.[7] From this perspective, the older version, putatively "the great wrath of Chemosh," was displaced by this more ambiguous version because the first was outmoded, inferior, and superstitious.[8]

4. He goes on to say: "The tale belongs to the popular prophetic cycle and uses the bald primitive lingo." Montgomery does not even mention what the "primitive implication" is. It appears almost a taboo subject for him, a coded way to erase the supernatural from the stories. Regarding such interpretation, Long observes: "The biblical narrator cannot have referred to the effective power of a non-Israelite god. . . . Thus 'great wrath' must have been associated with *Israel's* God, or with a *human* condition among Israel's troops. The logic inexorably demanded that Chemosh, or the mere possibility of Chemosh, be displaced in the narrative" (1991, 226–27).

5. Burns says this about the tendency of many to avoid the implications of this text: "The obscurity stems from a curiously persistent reluctance to accept what the text says" (1990, 191).

6. Long (1997, 225) cites Sanda, who suggests this original version. Burns and others, while accepting that the text means "the wrath of Chemosh," doubt that it ever needed or likely had such an addition (1990, 191). Long goes on to say, "The Old Testament is notoriously evasive when it comes to acknowledging the power of foreign gods. It was expedient to be reticent about the source of the anger."

7. Long observes, "By shrinking prophesied victory to indeterminate outcome, especially in a way that creates space for Chemosh, the narrator seems to equivocate, or rather, the mode of telling the tale undermines any simplistic appropriation of it" (1997, 227).

8. Nelson says: "The anticlimax undercuts the assumptions[:] . . . the traditional religious beliefs of humanity, their leaders, that one can actually know just what God is up to in any given set of events. The reader certainly has no idea what is going on, even after finishing the story. It undercuts all nationalistic and ethnocentric religion, the eternal human assumption that 'God is on our side.' In this case God seems to have been on both sides, or neither" (1987, 170).

Elisha's Prophecy: "Something Has Gone Wrong"

Elisha received his mantle of prophecy from Elijah, the self-proclaimed Yahwist, known for his extraordinary works of power and his violent hatred of Phoenician gods and their worshipers. When consulted in this battle to overtake Moab's capital city, Elisha gave strategic advice to the soldiers besieging the city. He thus brought the Israelites back from the brink of defeat. The water that he predicted would come flowed from Edom into their trenches and thus allowed them and their animals to have drink. Further, when the rising sun cast its oblique rays upon the water, the pools appeared red, drawing the Moabites into a disastrous raid on the alliance.

After the strategic instruction, Elisha predicted an Israelite victory: "This is only a trifle in the sight of the LORD, for he will also hand Moab over to you. You shall conquer every fortified city" (2 Kgs. 3:18–19).[9] This victory probably would have taken place had Mesha, in extremis, not slaughtered his son. So Elisha, mighty prophet of Yahweh, is proven wrong and impotent when confronted by the efforts of a foreign god on that god's own territory. This is not a matter of Elisha failing to discern Yahweh's word, or Yahweh equivocating with his word, as Philip Stern suggests, but rather it points to the failure of Yahweh's word because a different god, Chemosh, intervened. The writer of Kings seeks to establish the reliability of Yahweh's word, that Yahweh's word will always come to pass. Here it does not (Jones 1984, 391). As Bergen notes, "We are left with the uncomfortable sense that something has gone wrong" (Bergen 1992, 130).

Some interpreters, such as Philip Stern, claim that the wrath belongs to Yahweh alone. Stern argues that it could not be the wrath of Chemosh because foreign gods never experience emotions in the Hebrew Bible (1993, 11, citing Kaufmann). Rather, the word for "wrath," when used in contexts such as this, means the wrath of Yahweh.

There are in fact some good reasons to imagine Yahweh having cause against Israel. First and foremost, Yahweh appears to be angry with Jehoram, the king of Israel. Jehoram's mother, Jezebel, was a Phoenician princess who dedicated her efforts to instituting Baal worship in Israel, and Jehoram's father, Ahab, actively supported his wife's efforts (Stern 1993, 9). Jehoram had made some halfhearted efforts to put away the images that remained from his parents' religion, but such efforts did not endear him to Yahweh's prophet Elisha, who scorned him. "What have I to do with you? Go to your father's prophets

---

9. P. D. Stern suggests that Elisha (and Yahweh) had their fingers crossed when they predicted Israelite victory (1993, 7), that Elisha had only said that it was an easy thing for Yahweh to give the Moabites into his hand. He claims that Yahweh never actually *said* that he would do it, merely that he *could* do it with little effort. That seems a strained interpretation.

or to your mother's. . . . Were it not that I have regard for King Jehoshaphat of Judah, I would give you neither a look nor a glance" (2 Kgs. 3:13, 14).

Yahweh did not need any other excuses for his anger against Israel. One may only note the scorched-earth policy of Jehoram as he swept through the Moabite countryside: "The cities they overturned, and on every good piece of land everyone threw a stone, until it was covered; every spring of water they stopped up, and every good tree they felled" (2 Kgs. 3:25). This violated the holy war policy found in the book of Deuteronomy: "If you besiege a town for a long time, making war against it in order to take it, you must not destroy its trees by wielding an ax against them. Although you may take food from them, you must not cut them down. Are trees in the field human beings that they should come under siege from you?" (Deut. 20:19).[10] Finally, Israel's conquest of Moab goes against the fact of Yahweh's granting of the territory to Moab in Deuteronomy and Judges: "Should you not possess what your god Chemosh gives you to possess?" (Judg. 11:24). Jephthah seems to grant the god Chemosh an existence in Moab.

Jehoram's Reform: "Evil in the Sight of the LORD"

Jezebel, the queen mother, was still alive, and one could only imagine how she might have reacted when Jehoram, her son, removed the pillar of Baal that his father, Ahab, had made (2 Kgs. 3:2). According to the Deuteronomist, that was not enough. He still was regarded as having done "evil in the sight of Yahweh." Some traditions suggest that there was much reform that he left undone, perhaps out of respect or fear of his mother.

Jehoram did what any self-respecting king would do—he sought to restore the territory to his kingdom that had split away. He consulted an oracle before the battle. Perhaps it was the oracle that compelled him to go the roundabout way to reach Moab from the south through the wilderness area. But when the battle turned against him through lack of water, he complained, "Alas! The LORD has summoned us, three kings, only to be handed over to Moab" (v. 10). Jehoram clearly believed himself to be on a divine mission, and its imminent failure discouraged him, perhaps warning him away from his newfound faith.

If that was not enough, when the three kings (of Israel, Judah, and Edom) came down to Elisha so that he might inquire of Yahweh regarding

---

10. Cf. Deut. 2:9: "The LORD said to me: 'Do not harass Moab or engage them in battle, for I will not give you any of its land as a possession, since I have given Ar as a possession to the descendants of Lot.'"

the upcoming battle, the prophet scorned Jehoram (2 Kgs. 3:13, 14). There is nothing that can account for such hostility, save the previous history between the prophetic line of Elijah/Elisha and Jehoram's family in Israel. Jehoram's fault was his lineage. His efforts to become a king who served Yahweh had been met with rejection and ridicule. He had lost divine approval, even before he started. Had any one of the favored kings of Judah put away the pillar of Baal, launched a battle for national unity and regional hegemony, consulted a divine oracle, and followed a prophet's instructions implicitly, such a king would be regarded as one who "did what was right in the sight of the LORD all his days" (2 Kgs. 12:2). But because it was Jehoram, son of Jezebel and Ahab, he could do nothing right.

One notes the sense of halfhearted loyalty and bitter disappointment on the part of Jehoram, who tried to serve Yahweh. It certainly compares unfavorably to the fiery-hot devotion of King Mesha of Moab, who did not spare his own son from the demands of his god. Is it not ironic that in this story the devotion of a worshiper of Chemosh receives his blessing ultimately, while the efforts of Jehoram, while at first so promising, end in humiliating defeat?

This "supernatural" view inhabited a universe in which the gods Yahweh and Chemosh battled for dominance. A more "naturalistic" view would see behind the text a military defeat that was fueled by the superstitions of both sides. The troops of Moab were inspired by Mesha's sacrifice to redouble their efforts against the Israelite invaders; the Israelite troops were frightened by that selfsame sacrifice.[11] They lost heart and regarded themselves as being pursued by divine wrath.[12]

The Israelite Retreat: "Great Wrath Came upon Israel"

No soldier told another how he had felt that day. Even at the very beginning it felt odd to be in that place. Maybe diplomats and princes did not feel odd, but for common people of the land this territory smelled of unfamiliar power. The country seemed odd, somehow frightening. The natives spoke the same language, and lived in the same-shaped hovels, but

11. Montgomery observes: "The Israelites lost all heart in sight of the gruesome act. . . . The superstitious fears of the soldiery must have been much more alive in a land that was not their God's" (1950, 363–64).

12. Burns disagrees with this explanation: "Revulsion at human sacrifice was a most unlikely reaction. . . . To credit a group of soldiers, hardened to the grim facts of warfare and the rituals of human sacrifice, with a contemporary Western sensitivity and sentimentality, is naive and misleading" (1990, 193). Others have suggested that a plague swept through the camp (Jones 1984, 400), similar to the story of the Assyrian siege of Jerusalem.

there was a different smell to the place, a different expression to their eyes; even the way they stood bespoke of difference. The Israelites were on Chemosh's land. They were far from Yahweh, from the familiar shrines and temples back home. And what that young prophet ordered King Jehoram to do was difficult for any man to stomach: tearing down the cities, spending days carrying stones from the ruins and spreading them on fields, filling wells with them, fouling the place. They cut down all the trees and left the wood to rot there. They made the place a wasteland, while all the inhabitants hid.

And then at the very walls of Kir-haraseth, in sight of their prize (soon they could go home), the king did that thing, up there on the wall right by the gate, in plain sight of the Israelite troops.[13] Waves of fear and nausea swept through the Israelite encampment when they realized what the king was doing. They stood up in horror, oblivious to arrows and projectiles from the walls, and began screaming, first crying out for the king to stop and then just screaming. It was Chemosh walking among them, summoned by that horrid act. Some actually saw him, but others just felt the cold fear of him—his raw hatred of the Israelites. The officers could do nothing. The men, some not stopping to grab their gear, just ran. When the Moabites saw, they opened the gates and pursued the besieging army. Perhaps they yelled something like, "The sword of Mesha and of Chemosh!" But all that the Israelites yelled was "The wrath of Chemosh, the wrath of Chemosh!" and that is what the survivors said back in Israel when asked about the battle: "It was the wrath of Chemosh among us." Schwartz's general observations fit this passage well: "Making Yahwism the defining feature of Israel's collective identity seems to have come rather late in the long process of biblical composition, late enough to fail to completely eradicate the traces of polytheism found throughout the Bible" (Schwartz 1997, 31).

---

13. Both J. Robinson (1976, 37) and Gray (1970, 490) point to the cultic significance of the public sacrifice. It had to be seen by the Israelites in order to be effective, they say, to transfer the anger from the people of Moab to the Israelites. Both the Mesha inscription and 2 Kings 3 speak of wrath. Probably in 2 Kings 3 (as in the inscription without question) it is the wrath of Chemosh.

The Moabite Stone, on which was found the Mesha inscription, has remarkable similarities (and some differences as well) with the account of the war between Moab and Israel found in 2 Kings 3. In it, Mesha expresses his belief that his subjugation to Israel under its king Omri, along with Omri's son Ahab and his grandson Jehoram, was a result of the anger of the god Chemosh and that his overthrow of Israelite suzerainty was a result of Chemosh's anger redirected now against Israel (Pritchard 1969, 320–21; Matthews and Benjamin 1991, 112).

The first commandment, "You shall have no other gods before me," suggests the existence of multiple gods—not gods that exist only in the minds and beliefs of individual "pagans," but gods actually walking through the external world. This assumption (that multiple gods exist) underlies the first commandment. The Exodus narrative portrays the conflict between Yahweh and the gods of Egypt. Elijah's challenge was to the god Baal, who failed to deliver when called upon to send lightning upon the command of his priests. Does this passage suggest that the gods do not exist, or rather, that this particular god, Baal, is weak and ineffectual? Pretty much any time Israel encountered another nation or culture there was a struggle between two gods.

What astounds me is why Israelites would tell such a story, a story that would undermine Yahweh's claims (or their claims regarding Yahweh) to supremacy and exclusivity. The cosmological portrait of 2 Kings 3 conveys a universe in which there are many gods, whose strength is enhanced through the sacrifices of their followers—the more costly and personal the sacrifice, the greater the likelihood that a particular god will overpower competing gods. Along with Schwartz, I note that not all among the Israelite writers and storytellers subscribe to simple monotheism. At least some of the accounts represent a different point of view, and this in itself implies a plurality of positions within ancient Israel. This alternative to monotheism does not represent some ancient primitive form of Israelite religious belief, nor does it represent foreign belief. It is a native-born Israelite phenomenon.

Chapter 2

Miqreh

Happenstance in Ancient Israel

Ancient peoples accepted all disturbances in their lives as caused by the divine powers. This explains a great many phenomena in the Hebrew Bible and in other ancient Near Eastern literature. But I have always been fascinated with those ideas that live on the margins of acceptable thought; texts that contain those ideas might represent a minority opinion in ancient Israel. My attention was thereby drawn to a particular verse in 1 Samuel that concerns the ark, held in the Philistine camp: "And watch; if [the ark] goes up on the way to its own land, to Bethshemesh, then it is [Yahweh] who has done us this great harm; but if not, then we shall know that it is not his hand that struck us; it happened to us by chance" (6:9). The word translated "chance" is the Hebrew word *miqreh*. Here it clearly indicates a force potentially active in human affairs that is neither Yahweh, nor any other putative divine power.[1] Helmer Ringgren puts the significance of chance in its religious context:

> Things happen to man, they come upon him, so to speak, from the outside, and he has no power to change or to control them. It is to this part of his existence that man has to get into some kind of relationship, and the first step in this direction is an attempt to define what happens to him and to interpret it in a satisfactory way. It is here that the categories "god," "destiny," and "chance" enter the scene,

---

1. I find it astonishing that the monographs that focus on the ark narrative give little attention to this radical notion. They translate and move on (see, for example, Rost 1965; Schicklberger 1973; Campbell 1975; Miller and Roberts 1977).

13

depending on whether the events are derived from a personal power, an impersonal order, or no order at all. (Ringgren 1967, 7–8).[2]

I will explore in this chapter how this idea of a third force, neither Yahweh nor the other competing gods, appears in Hebrew literature, using as my central focus passages in which the word *miqreh* occurs. First, I will review the fundamental Hebrew theological position that Yahweh is the cause of all that occurs. Second, I will examine *miqreh* and other related words in the Hebrew text (those that share the same triliteral root). Third, I will focus upon the word *miqreh* in the two main contexts in which it appears: 1 Samuel 6 and throughout the book of Qoheleth (Ecclesiastes).

Divine Control of Human Events

Abraham's servant was sent on a complex mission in a distant land: to find a wife for his master's son. He prayed, "Grant me good fortune [*haqrēh-nā'*]" (Gen. 24:12).[3] The word translated "success" or "good fortune" is related to the word *miqreh*. This servant *expected* Yahweh to control events, and appropriately credits the deity for moving them in the proper direction.

Does God control all things? Ancient Israelites attributed sudden unexplained death to the wrath of Yahweh. The two hapless brothers Er and Onan are so afflicted. Er "was wicked in the sight of the LORD, and the LORD put him to death" (Gen. 38:7). The narrator makes this statement without explanation. "What [Onan] did was displeasing in the sight of the LORD, and he put him to death also" (Gen. 38:10). Although Onan's crime was apparent to the narrator (but not to the other characters), the story *assumes* that Yahweh caused his death.

Examples abound that support the Israelite assumption that Yahweh controlled unexplained catastrophes. When forty-two children are ripped apart by an angry bear, the narrator implies that Yahweh is responding to the impassioned curse of the balding prophet (2 Kgs. 2:23–25).[4] When Moses starts to die on the road to Egypt, the narrator informs us that Yahweh is trying to kill him (Exod. 4:24).[5] When David's son is stricken ill,

---

2. He goes on to note, "We disregard, then, the pure scientific, causal explanation" (ibid.).

3. A literal translation reads, "Please make it happen [for me]."

4. See Penchansky 1999, chapter 6.

5. A more mythological explanation of Exod. 4 is of course possible. A divine being might have appeared on the road and struck him down, but lacking any overt reference to such a being, the disease model provides a more useful explanatory function. See Penchansky 1999, chapter 5.

David accepts his son's death as the chastisement of God (2 Sam. 12:16). When one of the matriarchs cannot bear children, it is because Yahweh has closed her womb (Gen. 16:2).

Yahweh controls the simple events in life, especially the negative ones: the deaths, the illnesses, and the accidents. One must grasp this idea in order to understand the Hebrew belief that Yahweh controls everything. The writer of 1 and 2 Samuel hangs his entire theory of history on this one point—that Yahweh was in control, dispensing justice and retribution according to a rational, divine plan. Although some supposed divine actions seemed a little harsh or imbalanced, the Deuteronomist (the author of Samuel) remained confident in the mathematical purity of the divine will.

But did all Israelites without exception accept this interpretation of events? Occasional uses of *miqreh* and other words in the same language family suggest the possibility of random causation as a principle of interpretation. For a few writers at least, some things "just happen."

The Family of Words Related to *Miqreh*

Miqreh is formed from the triliteral root *qoph-resh-he* and shares with other members of that semantic family certain characteristics.[6] Among this family the verb *qārāh* appears most frequently in the Hebrew Bible, occurring twenty-seven times. It commonly communicates the idea of something happening to someone (e.g., Gen. 42:29: "When they came to their father Jacob in the land of Canaan, they told him all that had happened to them [*kol-haqōrōt*]"). The word might also refer to someone meeting someone (e.g., Exod. 3:18: "The LORD, the God of the Hebrews, has met [*niqrāh*] with us.").[7]

Most uses of the verb have this element in common: They emphasize the passive nature of the action with regard to the human subject. The person is met, or the event happens, *through no effort or intention on the part of the human subject*.[8] This uncontrolled event is in one place further emphasized by the use of the infinite absolute. A young man, an Amalekite,

6. I do not mean to imply that there is some kind of chronological development from the verb *qārāh* to the noun *miqreh*. Rather, there is a logical development that explains the appearance of a particular triliteral root within a relatively narrow body of texts. In fact, without much more evidence we cannot possibly know how the word developed.

7. This meaning is usually but not exclusively found in the Niphal (e.g., Exod. 3:18; Num. 23:3, 4, 15, 16), but see Deut. 25:17–18, where it occurs in the Qal.

8. Although in Exod. 3:18 and Num. 23:4 (and passim) "God *met* Balaam," the emphasis of the sentence is on Balaam's inability to control the circumstances of this meeting. Syntactically, the subject (God) is active, but the literary context still demands a passive intent to the verb.

in an effort to endear himself to the new king, David, reports that he has encountered King Saul, David's enemy, dying on the battlefield. Denying any intentional treason toward the old king, he asserts "By chance I happened to be [*niqrō³ niqrêtî*] on Mount Gilboa."⁹ Although his forceful semantic style was unsuccessful (David had him executed), his syntax indicates the passive character of the word *qārāh*, emphasized through this use of the infinite absolute.¹⁰ The Amalekite claims in the strongest way available to him in the language that he had absolutely no intention to betray King Saul.

Sometimes, though not often, the word will imply a positive occurrence, as in the prayer of Abraham's servant mentioned above.¹¹ But more commonly the word will have a neutral sense, often given a negative twist through the insertion of a negative subject or explanatory clause: "Remember . . . how [Amalek] attacked you [*qārkā*] on the way" (Deut. 25:17–18), or Jacob's sorrowful speech concerning Benjamin, "If you take this one also from me, and harm comes to him [*wĕqārāhû*], you will bring down my gray hairs in sorrow to Sheol" (Gen. 44:29).¹²

Two other occurrences of the root strongly suggest negative experiences. *Qāreh*, a noun, is used once, only in Deuteronomy. The RSV translates it, "If there is among you any man who is not clean by reason of what chances to him by night [*miqrēh-lāylāh*], then he shall go outside the camp" (Deut. 23:11; Eng. 23:10). Most commentators agree with the NRSV, which translates the phrase "because of a nocturnal emission," what in plain English we call a "wet dream" (see Brown, Driver, and Briggs 1978, 899).

Miqreh in 1 Samuel

The noun *miqreh* occurs twice in 1 Samuel. In 20:26, King Saul, trying to account for David's absence, speculates, "Something has befallen him [*miqreh hû³*]." Saul thereby indirectly suggests that David has had a wet

---

9. A literal translation reads, "Meeting, I did meet . . ."

10. Note also the double use of the form in Ruth 2:3.

11. Other possible occurrences of *qārāh* meaning "good fortune" are Ruth 2:3 (but see the discussion of *miqreh*), 2 Sam. 1:6, and the passages relating to Balaam (Num. 3). Other than the Gen. 24 passage, the other positive inferences are decidedly vague.

12. See also 1 Sam. 28:10, where "punishment" is the subject; Gen. 42:29, where the brothers report on their frightening experience in Egypt; and Esth. 4:7 and 6:13, where Mordecai and Haman, respectively, report on the negative experiences inflicted on them.

dream, rendering him unclean and unfit to attend the religious feast. Likewise, the occurrence of *miqreh* in Ruth 2:3 is a mere adaptation of the verbal form: "So she went. She came and gleaned in the field behind the reapers. As it happened, she came [*wayyiqer miqrehā*] to the part of the field belonging to Boaz." Note also the use of the verb *qarah* with the noun *miqreh* to emphasize the unexpected and fortuitous turn of events.

However, the occurrences of *miqreh* in 1 Samuel 6 suggest unique theological overtones not present in chapter 20. The Philistines, having captured the ark, suffer a series of disasters. The "hand of Yahweh" is heavy upon them, upon their gods, and upon their land (see 6:5). The five Philistine kings consult their theological experts, the priests and diviners, with a twofold request. They desire first to determine reliably by means of divination (Campbell 1975, 103) that it was indeed Yahweh who had afflicted them, and second to determine what exactly would be the best way to remove the curse, if indeed these disasters were brought upon them by the Israelite god.[13] The priests and diviners offer a single solution to answer both of these questions.[14] They construct the circumstances by which an offering would be given to placate Yahweh, but *only if Yahweh were truly the culprit*. Miller and Roberts observe:

> The reason for all these careful preparations is indicated in vs. 9. The Philistines had assumed that the reason for the plague was Yahweh's anger, but without divine revelation they could not be sure. What had befallen the Philistines could have been *fortuitous* [emphasis added]. Thus the Philistines take these precautions to make certain that it really was Yahweh who was responsible for the plague. (Miller and Roberts 1977, 56)

If Yahweh did not do it, then some other power did. The Philistine priests would have to keep searching until they found the explanation for the diseases.

The priests and diviners directed that two milk cows deprived of their calves would be yoked to a cart containing the offerings for Yahweh. Were

13. Miller and Roberts break down the second question (which actually occurs first in the narrative) into two parts: (1) How do we get rid of the ark, and (2) what should we send with it? (1977, 52). See also Campbell (1975, 110–13).

14. Rost sees the multiplicity of questions as indications of a corrupt text (1965, 129). See Miller and Roberts (1977, 103) for persuasive counterarguments.

Yahweh uninvolved in the Philistine plagues, the cows would naturally return to their stables to feed their hungry calves and relieve the pressure of stored milk. But if the cows pulled the cart to the borders of Yahweh's own land in spite of their discomfort at their calves' bleating, then "it is [Yahweh] who has done us this great harm" (1 Sam. 6:9).

The diviners also presented a hypothetical alternative. What would be the theological conclusion if the cows were to return to their stables where their calves are eager to nurse? "But if not, then we shall know that it is not [Yahweh's] hand that struck us; it happened to us by chance [*miqreh hûʾ hāyāh lānû*]."[15] The contrast is established between "the hand of Yahweh" and *miqreh*. Yahweh's activity is not opposed to the activity of some other god. The priests and diviners clearly say that the Philistine gods themselves are being afflicted in this plague. The unfortunate statue of Dagon has fallen down twice, the second time losing his head and hands. The priests offer a third alternative: neither Yahweh, nor any other god, but rather *miqreh*.

One must thereby tentatively conclude that Israelites were acquainted with the idea that random events occur independent of the gods. However, this word, *miqreh*, and this concept, chance or fate, are placed in the mouths of the "uncircumcised Philistines," thus rendering this a seditious idea, an *uncircumcised* idea. Further, the narrator informs us that *miqreh* is not the cause of the Philistine plagues.[16] The cows go directly to Beth-shemesh, thus proving Yahweh's involvement. The story eliminates the possibility of *miqreh* as a factor in the cows' behavior.

Miqreh in Qoheleth

The door has been opened. An alien concept, that of blind chance causing certain events, has been introduced, and we search diligently through the Hebrew Bible for any further evidence for such an idea. We find the word *miqreh* occurring seven times in Qoheleth,[17] a book with many ideas alien to the rest of the Bible. The preacher, who narrates most of the book, answers the question: Is there any purpose in being wise?

---

15. A literal translation reads, "It surely will be *miqreh* to us."

16. The purpose of this portion of the ark narrative is to demonstrate "the superiority of the God of Israel over the national God of the Philistines. Such is the reality which the author of the Samuel narrative sought to demonstrate" (Delcor 1964, 148).

17. *Miqreh* occurs ten times in the Hebrew Bible as a whole, including twice in 1 Samuel (6:9 and 20:26) and once in Ruth (2:3).

The wise have eyes in their head, but fools walk in darkness. Yet I perceived that the same fate [*šemmiqreh*][18] befalls [*yiqreh*] all of them. Then I said to myself, "What happens to the fool [*kĕmiqrēh haksîl*] will happen to me [*yiqrēnî*] also. (Qoh. 2:14–15)[19]

For the fate [*miqreh*] of humanity [*bĕnê-hā᾿ādām*] and the fate [*miqreh*] of the beasts is the same [*ûmiqreh ᾿eḥād*]; as one dies, so dies the other. (Qoh. 3:19)

The same fate [*miqreh ᾿eḥād*] comes to all, to the righteous and the wicked. . . . As are the good, so are the sinners. . . . This is an evil in all that happens under the sun, that the same fate [*miqreh ᾿eḥād*] comes to everyone. (Qoh. 9:2–3)

These three texts tell us similar things. *Miqreh* renders the distinctions between the wise and the foolish, between the human and the animal, between the righteous and the wicked, meaningless. What is the use, if all face the same inevitable *miqreh*, that is, a sure and certain death? For Qoheleth, *miqreh* undermines the very idea that religious effort bears fruit.

By equalizing all human categories, Qoheleth produces a sense of futility. He neutralizes the value of wisdom and moral choice. Although he does not directly challenge the reality of divine existence, he undermines the efficacy of the divine power at every turn. Therefore, human efforts to placate that divine power are doomed to failure, or at least sentenced to ambiguity. The authors of Samuel found God faithful and dependable, but *miqreh* is inscrutable and can strike out at any moment.

The idea of *miqreh* in Qoheleth preserves an element of mystery. It points, as Kees Bolle suggests in a different context, to "something higher and more powerful than what tradition allowed or was capable of understanding. . . . [It indicates] the desire to point to and name the power beyond what the tradition tolerates" (Bolle 1987, 296).[20] However, the concept of chance challenges a basic idea of monotheism. As Yusa observes, "The Christian stance on chance varies somewhat: whereas Augustine denied any possibility of chance or fortune in view of all-controlling providence,

18. The preformative *shem* seems to serve no grammatical function. See Kautzsch and Cowley (1982, 237).

19. A literal translation reads, "As *miqreh* to the fool, so it will also happen to me."

20. Bolle notes a shift from this position in later developments: "In the religion of Israel, the basic pattern to be continued in Judaism, Christianity, and Islam had already clearly emerged. . . . The most general tendency is to associate destiny with the will of God" (1987, 295).

Thomas Aquinas admitted chance with the providential scheme" (Yusa 1987, 193). It is a *subversive* idea meant to challenge the ancient defenders of the Israelite religion. According to Bolle, "Generally, the biblically rooted religions, Judaism, Christianity, and Islam, looked askance at every semblance of a fate that could be ascertained apart from God" (Bolle 1987, 294).

The concept of fate sets up a number of dichotomies: (1) Do the gods control fate, or are they controlled by fate? (2) Is fate a blind force, or does it have a godlike personality? (3) Can humans know their fate, or is it inscrutable? (4) Does fate give freedom, or does it deny human power of choice? Ringgren observes: "The belief in a personal determiner of destiny produces religious behavior, while the belief in an impersonal Fate does not. But the problem is complicated by the fact that both of these attitudes seem to occur together in one and the same religion, even in one and the same person" (1967, 8). The concept of "fate" has existed in most cultures, and always seems to contain some ambiguity as to whether human destiny is in the hands of the gods or is somehow independent of them (Bolle 1987, 292–96).

These usages of *miqreh* in Qoheleth differ significantly from the passage about the ark in 1 Samuel 6. Whereas in the ark narrative most English translations represent *miqreh* by the English word "chance," meaning a random uncaused event, the context in Qoheleth demands the translation "fate," meaning that which inevitably happens to a person.[21] Qoheleth associates fate with the inevitability of death. Bolle defines fate as "the idea that everything in human lives, in society, in the world itself takes place according to a set immutable pattern" (1987, 290).[22] Yusa contends, "Chance and fate—these initially contradictory notions are but two counter-interpretations of the experience of unexpected coincidence or happenings that seem arbitrary but nevertheless have a decisive impact on one's life and in some cases totally change it" (Yusa 1987, 194).

I hold, however, that the two contexts of *miqreh*, in 1 Samuel and in Qoheleth, are not homonyms. Although no one English word can carry the meanings of both these contexts, in Hebrew both contexts speak of

---

21. Whybray sees the use of *miqreh* here and elsewhere in Qoheleth as less theologically charged than I do. He states, "Fate in Qoheleth's thought, as elsewhere in the Old Testament, does not signify an impersonal or malignant force but is a 'neutral' term signifying simply what happens" (1989, 58). But he is undoubtedly correct when he argues that the term *miqreh* betrays no Greek influence, as was previously believed (see also 79 and 141).

22. He goes on to say that "the notion of fate . . . always retains a basic element of mystery" (1987, 290).

this third force—events over which divine power and human effort have limited control. In 1 Samuel, the *randomness* of the action is in the foreground. In Qoheleth, the *negative* nature of the event is in the foreground. In both senses of *miqreh*, mystery is an important aspect. In both contexts, the word implies the accident, the uncaused event. Ringgren notes:

> If the power of destiny is regarded as impersonal, it is impossible to enter into any kind of relationship with it. The decree of destiny cannot be changed or averted, and it is no use praying or offering sacrifices, for there is no one to hear or to receive and to react. On the other hand, if man's fate is decreed by a god, it is possible to enter into relationship with him, and sacrifices, prayer and obedience may be thought to avert an evil destiny or create a good one, and so forth. (1967, 8)

We might, therefore, draw the following conclusions. First, the idea of events uncaused by Yahweh existed as a concept in ancient Israel. Second, this idea of a third force was unpopular in Israel and thereby suppressed. Bolle notes that in most cultures there is a deliberate ambivalence between two contrary notions of this third force: fate as under the control of the gods, or fate as beyond divine control. He says, "Such ambivalence is not mere intellectual uncertainty but often an intentional compromise of distinct views, each of which is unassailable" (1987, 292). When this notion does appear, it is placed in the mouths of the most theologically suspect individuals: the "uncircumcised Philistines," who engage in incorrect speculation, and the pessimist Qoheleth, whose utterances border on heresy.

Third, we might speak of the importance of this concept in Israelite thinking. The idea that one can explain all events by claiming God as the cause for everything produces no end of theological problems. It brings one to question both divine goodness and divine ability. The most common expression of the problem follows this line of reasoning: If God is both good and all-powerful, why does God let evil happen in the world? The problem of evil cannot be adequately addressed by the traditional theological explanation.[23]

---

23. The book of Job, while not offering *miqreh* as an explanatory principle, grapples with the question of the orderliness of the divine will. Job never finds out the origin of his curse, and the suggestion of a wager between Yahweh and the Satan is so patently odd that it is not taken seriously as a theological option in the rest of the book. What remains, by default, is *miqreh*. See Penchansky 1989.

Finally, it is with *miqreh* that we may find some point of contact between the ancient Israelites and ourselves. In their world they believed that God caused everything. In our culture we are told to "take responsibility" for whatever comes our way. We cause everything, some tell us, even our sicknesses. It therefore becomes incumbent upon both cultures to occasionally affirm with another ancient theologian that "neither this man, nor his parents sinned," and that "the rain falls on the just and the unjust"—in short, that some things just happen.

Chapter 3

Bĕnê ʾElōhîm

The Divine Council in the Hebrew Bible

At least some in Israel described Yahweh as the ruler in a heavenly council. In this chapter, I explore instances in which the divine council appears. The authors of the Bible had an ambiguous relationship with the notion of an Israelite pantheon—sometimes ignoring it, sometimes writing diatribes against it, and sometimes flattening out the individuality of its members. Some texts make the *bĕnê ʾelōhîm*[1] a faceless mask with no independent will, serving only as messengers for Yahweh. For example, the psalmist exclaims:

> Bless the LORD, all his hosts,
>   his ministers that do his will.
>   (Ps. 103:21)

> Praise him, all his angels;
>   Praise him, all his host!
>   (Ps. 148:2)

"Host" and "angels" are both references to members of the council. The first stresses their military function, the second their role as messengers.

Divine beings inhabit the heavenly realm, beings distinct from Yahweh, Israel's God. The character of these beings varies widely, and they carry a number of different names. One of those names is "angel." These beings, who live in a heavenly realm, have great powers, knowledge, and

---

1. In the Hebrew Bible, this phrase frequently appears as *bĕnê haʾelōhîm* with no difference in meaning.

immortality. In any other culture they would be called "gods." We do not think of them in that way because we have been trained to read the Bible with a monotheistic lens.[2] This tradition of a divine council, though of great antiquity, remained a vibrant belief in ancient Israel throughout its history, at least among certain groups.

Groups of divine beings meet together to conduct business. We commonly translate *běnê* in other contexts as "sons of . . ." *ʾElōhîm* becomes in English "God" or "gods." But the phrase *běnê ʾelōhîm* does not mean God's offspring, "the sons of God"; rather, the words signify "members of Yahweh's council." Alternatively, "sons of" might mean, "having the common identity of." Thus, *běnê ʾelōhîm* would then mean, "those that have the common characteristics of divine beings; members of the same species." One gets a glimpse, then, of what must have been a thoroughgoing, multifaceted pantheon in ancient Israel. What remains of this pantheon today are the angels who inhabit the sacred universes of Judaism, Christianity, and Islam, who do the bidding of God.[3]

The Hebrew word *ʾelōhîm* also frequently refers generically to the Israelite god, and is then ordinarily rendered as "God." But the ending to the word, *im*, is plural, and so *ʾelōhîm* can mean "gods."[4] It can also be used as a superlative. For instance, whereas *rûaḥ ʾelōhîm* (Gen. 1:2) might mean "the wind of God," "spirit of God," or "divine wind," it might also be translated as a superlative: "a very great wind."

The phrase *běnê ʾelōhîm* then refers to a class of beings. They are divine beings, inhabitants of the realm of heaven.[5] Also resonant within this phrase is the notion that *ʾelōhîm* (God) rules over this group, a kind of divine council, and that the term *běnê* makes them his underlings, his cabinet.[6]

---

2. Smith (2001) takes this position. Although he says that the individuality of the members of the pantheon drops out, the ancient text editors preserved a few stories where the particular different beings remained.

3. Some of these gods were demoted to the status of angels. Smith supports this: "Certainly angels are not regarded in later tradition as gods. Instead, they are powers that act only in the name of their patron god and only thanks to the power of that deity" (2001, 49–50).

4. When the Hebrew verb is masculine singular, *ʾelōhîm* is translated "God." When the verb is masculine plural, in English it is translated "gods."

5. We see a similar phenomenon in the phrase *běnê Yiśrāʾēl*, which does not mean "sons of Israel," but rather "Israelites."

6. *ʾElōhîm* does double duty in this instance, representing both the class of divine beings and the leader of divine beings, the head of the council. *ʾel* is an alternative Hebrew name for God, and in ancient Canaanite mythology El was the head of the divine pantheon.

Genesis 6

At the beginning of the flood narrative (Gen. 6–9) there is an unusual story:

> When people began to multiply on the face of the ground, and daughters were born to them, the sons of God [*běnê ʾelōhîm*] saw that they were fair; and they took wives for themselves of all that they chose. . . . The Nephilim were on the earth in those days—and also afterward—when the sons of God [*běnê ʾelōhîm*] went in to the daughters of humans, who bore children to them. These were the heroes that were of old, warriors of renown. (Gen. 6:1–4)

In its present context, the behavior of the human women provides the final provocation and therefore justifies Yahweh's destruction of the earth by flood, but the story is much earlier than its context. The original tale divides into three parts: (1) The *běnê ʾelōhîm* see and desire the women; (2) they have sex with the women; and (3) the women bear them children, presumably the giants, the Nephilim.

Many have marveled that such an odd story, so much like Greek mythology, finds a place in the Bible. In it the *běnê ʾelōhîm* act wickedly.[7] In its original form, the narrative appears to have been an etiology (origin story) for the presence of the Nephilim (giants) in the land.[8] It was not originally a story about human corruption, not a story which concludes that "all human imagination is only evil continually" (Gen. 6:5) Rather, it is about a group of women who were raped by divine beings who came out of the sky or down from the mountains. (The *běnê ʾelōhîm* had sexually desired the humans: "The *běnê ʾelōhîm* saw that they were fair" and so "they took . . . all that they chose" [Gen. 6:2]).

An immeasurable power differential exists between the humans and the *ʾelōhîm*, who did not need the human women's cooperation. This is similar to myths from other cultures that describe instances of divine rape. The *ʾelōhîm* forced the women to become receptacles for divine semen. What are the defenses of human women against the powerful maleness of these deities?

---

7. Some have suggested that *běnê ʾelōhîm* means here (and nowhere else) "human men," as *bānôt haʾādām* (literally, "daughters of *ʾādām*") means "human women," and that the construct "of *ʾelōhîm*" means "good humans," and "of *ʾādām*" means "bad humans." There is no precedent or justification for using either *ʾelōhîm* or *ʾādām* in these ways.

8. This is the way an etiology might have worked:
"Where did these giants, the Nephilim, come from?"
"Once upon a time, divine beings came from heaven and stole our women. . . ."

Never again do we find a biblical text that regards the members of the divine council sexually. This is the only place in the Bible where the *ʾelōhîm* are described as having male genitals and potent semen. So dramatically did later traditions reject the idea of sexual *ʾelōhîm* that Jesus addressed the topic in the New Testament. He asserted that dead humans "neither marry nor are given in marriage, but are like angels in heaven" (Matt. 22:30). In other words, in the first century, the angels were not regarded as sexual beings. But in the older text, these beings act to pursue their own desires and satisfaction. They have physical bodies, experience the desires of the body, and have the physical means to satisfy that desire. Nowhere else will we see these figures so humanlike.

As in no place else in the Hebrew Bible, here we see an extreme example of the *ʾelōhîm* acting like the gods in other Mediterranean stories, acting willful and sexual. Their behavior is sufficient cause (in the present version) for Yahweh to despair of the humans and to will their destruction.[9] One wonders why the final editor did not soften the intense presence of the *ʾelōhîm*, or leave them out altogether. Apparently the story ran so deep in the consciousness and memory of the people that the monotheistic editor did not dare remove it.[10]

Job

Job offers a more difficult case. How we read the introduction to the book depends upon whether or not we regard the Satan as one of the *běnê ʾelōhîm*. (The Hebrew text adds the definite article "the" because here it is a title, not a name [*hašaṭan*]. The Hebrew verb *satan* means "to oppose," and thus in the noun form it becomes "the adversary," "one who opposes.") The *běnê ʾelōhîm* assemble before Yahweh in the book of Job, presumably for administrative reasons (chapters 1 and 2). The Satan comes also, whether as a full-fledged member or as an interloper the text does not say. "One day the heavenly beings [*běnê ʾelōhîm*] came to present themselves before the LORD, and Satan [*ha-šaṭan*] also came among them" (Job 1:6).

9. Although I find inevitable the conclusion that the Nephilim are the offspring of the gods and the humans, the text does not actually ever say that. There just happened to be giants in the neighborhood directly after the divine-human sexual activity. The text as it stands is exceedingly skittish about actually describing the biological result of the *ʾElōhîm*-human sexual union.

10. The later editor, it seems, placed this much older story in the larger context of the flood, so that the polytheistic elements of the story might not be obvious or disturbing.

On the surface of things, the Satan does the same kinds of things as the *běnê ʾelōhîm* in other passages. He brings information to Yahweh, helps Yahweh deliberate what to do, and he carries out Yahweh's will in the human realm. The *běnê ʾelōhîm* themselves do nothing in the story except assemble twice at the appointed time. Only the Satan and Yahweh have speaking parts. The narrator reduces the *běnê ʾelōhîm* into a backdrop.[11]

Yahweh and the Satan make a bet. The Satan challenges Yahweh that if they took all the blessings away from righteous Job, the poor saintly man would "curse you to your face" (Job 1:11). Yahweh bets that Job would indeed remain steadfast. In chapter 2, Yahweh complains, "You made me afflict him [Job] for no good reason" (Job 2:3). With these words, Yahweh accuses the Satan of tricking him. How might we discern the Satan's intention? Does he want to prove that Job serves Yahweh for gain? If that is the case, then Yahweh wins the competition between them. Or did the Satan intend to trick Yahweh into destroying his favored servant? In either case, the book portrays a supernatural being in the heavenly court opposed to human well-being and capable of deceiving Yahweh, his boss, in order to override Yahweh's divine protection of Job.

Psalm 89

Psalm 89 offers a different perspective on the divine council. The psalmist draws up a polemic that proves that Yahweh surpasses the members of the divine council in every respect. Although this psalm too represents the *běnê ʾelōhîm* as a faceless group, they clearly exist independently from Yahweh. The following offers some good examples:

> Let the heavens praise your wonders, O LORD,
>   your faithfulness in the assembly of the holy ones.
> For who in the skies can be compared to the LORD?
>   Who among the heavenly beings [*běnê ʾelōhîm*] is like the LORD,
> a God feared in the council of the holy ones,
>   great and awesome above all that are around him?
> O LORD God of hosts,
>   who is as mighty as you, O LORD?
>
> (vv. 5–8)

11. See P. L. Day 1986 for a good overview. See also Penchansky 1989, 56–61.

Note the parallel between a number of terms used in Psalm 89: (1) the council of the holy ones and those that are around Yahweh; (2) the hosts of heaven ("LORD God of hosts") and the ones in the skies; (3) the ones in heaven and the assembly of the holy ones.

The poet wrote this psalm as a polemic to attack the practice of worshiping the hosts of heaven by presenting them as subservient in every way to Yahweh. The divine beings, the congregation of holy ones, praise Yahweh. They cannot be compared to Yahweh, nor does any of them resemble Yahweh. Rather, they fear him.

Micaiah Ben Imlah (1 Kings 22)

In the Hebrew Bible, only in 1 Kings 22 do we actually witness a debate that takes place in the divine council. The council is mostly part of the faceless throng, but in 1 Kings 22 individual members of the host of heaven separate into various "spirits" with differing opinions. Prophets have access to the divine realm. In this passage we actually see the prophet eavesdropping on a meeting of the divine council.[12]

A king requires divine information, and prophets with access to the divine council are a source for that information. This particular king, Ahab, has inquired of Yahweh whether or not he should fight a battle the following day. His court prophets encourage him to do it. They tell him what he wants to hear: "Go up; for the LORD will give it into the hand of the king" (1 Kgs. 22:6). Under threat of punishment if he dissents, Micaiah the prophet agrees with the battle plan and makes the required speech. He proclaims, "Go up and triumph; the LORD will give it into the hand of the king" (v. 15). But the king insists, "How many times must I make you swear to tell me nothing but the truth in the name of the LORD?" (v. 16). The true message would be that King Ahab was doomed. But after dumping that on the king, Micaiah describes a discussion, a kind of legislative debate that goes on among the "host of heaven," the "spirits":

> I saw the LORD sitting on his throne, with all the host of heaven [ṣĕbāʾ hašāmayîm] standing beside him to the right and to the left of him. And the LORD said, "Who will entice Ahab, so that he may go up and fall at Ramoth-gilead?" Then one said one thing, and another said another, until a spirit came forward and stood before the LORD, say-

---

12. Isaiah 6 might be another such instance, but Yahweh alone consults with the prophet in this passage. The cherubim (heavenly beings) worship but do not speak.

ing, "I will entice him." "How?" the LORD asked him. He replied, "I will go out and be a lying spirit in the mouth of all his prophets." (vv. 19–22)

The suggestion Yahweh favors (the only one mentioned) is that one of the host of heaven, one of the spirits, would inspire the prophets to lie to the king.

Micaiah claims to have actually witnessed the policy discussion taking place in heaven, where Yahweh first asked for ideas and then for volunteers. The people in his council in this story are called spirits. Yahweh serves as a chair of the council, getting feedback from underlings, then making a decision. Subsequently, he delegates the actual carrying out of policy. So in a sense the prophets spoke lies at Yahweh's behest. A "lying spirit" dispatched from the divine council brings the false message. The king goes into battle the next day, is shot by a random arrow, and bleeds to death in his chariot.

First-Person Plural Address in Genesis 1, 2–3, 10

When we see the consultation that takes place in the divine council, the divine "we" and "us" at the beginning of Genesis begins to make sense. Every year students ask me, "Who is God talking to when he says 'Let *us* make *ʾādām* in our image'?" (Gen. 1:26).[13] The Christian tradition has sometimes suggested that here we see a discussion between the members of the Holy Trinity. The story makes more sense if we imagine Yahweh consulting his *běnê ʾelōhîm*, his divine council. The appearance of these beings (although nearly invisible in the first three chapters of Genesis) indicates that they were present at the very beginning of creation in a consultative role.

In the garden of Eden story, Yahweh is called *Yahweh ʾelōhîm*.[14] This phrase suggests a range of possible meanings. It might mean that Yahweh is the leader of the band of *ʾelōhîm*, or else that Yahweh is a god from the class of beings named *ʾelōhîm*. This two-word title might also mean both of these things. In either case, the term *ʾelōhîm* qualifies Yahweh, indicating what category of being Yahweh is.

Yahweh places the two trees in the garden for the benefit of the *ʾelōhîm*. I infer this because Yahweh did not allow the humans to eat from them,

---

13. *ʾādām* is a Hebrew transliteration that refers to human beings without reference to gender.

14. See Penchansky 1999, chapter 1.

and the trees impart qualities by which the gods are identified. Apparently, the ʾelōhîm regularly consume the fruit provided by the two trees. Yahweh intended neither for the humans. The tree of life imparted to the ʾelōhîm eternal life or immortality. The other tree, the tree of the knowledge of good and evil, imparted divine insight and gave the ʾelōhîm their unique knowledge.[15] When humans eat the fruit from that tree, Yahweh addresses his council with the problem: "See, the man has become like one of *us*, knowing good and evil" (Gen. 3:22).

The ʾelōhîm therefore conspired to drive the humans out of the garden before they gained access to the tree of life. If, in addition to gaining divine knowledge they would live forever, then there would be nothing to distinguish the ʾelōhîm from the humans.[16] Such a prospect was unacceptable to *Yahweh ʾelōhîm*, their leader. As a result of human impudence, he drove the first couple from the garden and forced them to fend for themselves. Apparently, divine prerogatives must be preserved at all costs!

Two things about the ʾelōhîm in the garden of Eden story deserve our attention. First, when Yahweh says, "See, the man has become like one of us," the negative import of that line is powerful—the ʾelōhîm are horrified at the prospect of sharing their realm with the humans. Yahweh, however, includes himself in the "us." He is one of the ʾelōhîm. Second, Yahweh questions the ʾelōhîm and consults with them about how to dispose of his creation. Therefore, they must have wisdom upon which Yahweh depends.

I thus note the two chief characteristics that distinguish the ʾelōhîm from other types of beings: divine life (immortality) and divine knowledge. The remainder of the human story following the expulsion from the garden might then be understood as an eternal, generation-by-generation quest to recover the tree of life, which is finally granted to the humans at the end of the age in both the Jewish and the Christian traditions.

Other Divine Beings in Genesis

One more story fills out the picture. Three men approach Abraham. "He looked up and saw three men standing near him" (Gen. 18:2). Abraham identifies one of them as Yahweh. The narrator calls the other two "angels" (19:1). Yahweh sends them to Sodom as his eyes and ears, to investigate

15. Some have seen this tree as imparting moral knowledge, but more likely it indicates the scope of knowledge, the entirety of things that can be known. "From good to evil," we might translate, as in English one might say "from A to Z," or "from top to bottom."

16. See Barr 1993, especially chapter 1.

firsthand the charges against Sodom and the cities of the plain. Upon first glance, these two men are indistinguishable from Yahweh, and Abraham cannot distinguish them from human beings. The three together are characterized as men (*ʾănāšîm*), and presumably look just like men walking down the road. The two with Yahweh are called "men" five times and "angels" twice. These two speak only through Yahweh.

The three men set out to Sodom because, as Yahweh says, "*I* must go down and see . . ." (18:21). Abraham serves as their guide: "[He] went with them to set them on their way" (v. 16). In verse 22 we are told, "So the men turned from there, and went toward Sodom, while Abraham remained standing before the LORD." Yahweh says that he "must go down and see," but then remains to discuss matters with Abraham, who stands submissively. The other two men must serve as extensions of Yahweh's eyes, providing a way for him to be in more than one place at once.

Although the men are neither named nor described, they remain distinguishable from Yahweh. They make decisions and act independently. They participate in specific ways in the narrative: carrying messages from Yahweh, physically pulling Lot, Abraham's nephew, out of danger, protecting Lot's family by striking with blindness the abusive mob, and forcing the family out of the city. However, they never function or speak singly. In 19:21, "they" becomes "he" when Lot asks the angels to let his family stay in Zoar instead of in the hills. So the two men/angels who accompanied Yahweh are less faceless, more specific and particular than the amorphous *běnê ʾelōhîm* in Job, but they never completely individuate.

In these passages, one gets a glimpse of what must have been a thoroughgoing, multifaceted pantheon in ancient Israel. This vibrant tradition of the divine council in the Hebrew Bible portrays the members of the divine council (dwelling upon an Israelite Mount Olympus) as independent, divine beings.

As we approach the Greek period, two things had changed regarding them. First, the Israelite God, Yahweh, took the dominant position in Israel as the only true God. Earlier, Yahweh stood in the midst of a wide group of competing gods, albeit the most powerful among them. The second change is the dramatic expansion of the role of the angel. Previously, angels were treated collectively. With the exception of "the Satan," who had an individual title, all were named as a group (*běnê ʾelōhîm*, spirits, host of heaven, holy ones, etc.), at least until the second temple period. Now they began to obtain individual names and gradations of power.

At this point, the name Yahweh drops out of the vocabulary, being too holy to pronounce. Perhaps also the sacred name had outlived its usefulness. One only needs personal names to distinguish between objects of the same class, human beings for instance. So when the class of "gods" only contained one member, the need for a personal name no longer existed. How unusual that Israelites should change in these two ways at the same time. They seem to conflict with each other, with one movement to reduce the category "god" to describe only one being, and the other to expand and differentiate the population of heavenly personalities.

The Jews in the late Persian and Greek periods developed a unique strategy for reconciling this conflict. They changed the word *ᵓelōhîm* and the concepts represented by that word. Previously, the word shifted between three definitions: (1) a generic term for a being of the heavenly class; (2) a particular representative of that class, a god; and (3) a generic term for the God of Israel. Henceforth, only the third meaning would be permitted. Now *ᵓelōhîm* must only mean the one and only divine being, infinite, with no beginning or end. Therefore, these other beings, inhabitants of heaven, who would qualify as "gods" in any other culture, here are only angels. Thus, Yahweh merged with the philosophical notion of the absolute, a trend that had begun long before but begins to be realized at this moment.

Chapter 4

The Dissolution of the Divine Council

"You shall have no other gods before me."

This command underpins the biblical claim of monotheism. Yet, contrary to popular understanding, it assumes the existence of other gods. The key phrase "before me"[1] might be best understood as "in my presence," and has the further sense of "in my presence to perform a religious activity such as sacrifice or worship." The language strictly prohibits bringing other gods around when Yahweh is worshiped. It does not prohibit having other gods or worshiping them in some other place.

This command assumes that other gods exist and that they may be worshiped, only not in Yahweh's presence. Later communities in Israel reinterpreted this command. They believed that this text denied the very existence of other gods. I have demonstrated that Israel believed in many gods. However, such belief risked opposition from significant and powerful factions within the nation. Radical monotheists in Israel spoke of other gods in two ways: (1) They gave a mythic account of how Yahweh cast down the other gods from their high offices, and (2) they mocked and satirized the worship of other gods.

The Decline of the Divine Council

As I noted in chapter 3, students often ask me to whom God is speaking in Genesis 2 when he says, "Let *us* make humankind in *our* image." After surveying the various options, I always lay out the strongest of them, that

---

1. A more literal translation would read, "to my face" (ʿal-pānāy).

Yahweh Elohim was consulting with his council of advisors, the ʾelōhîm. When the Satan appears before Yahweh in the book of Job, he comes during the assembly of the běnê ʾelōhîm, the ʾelōhîm beings. Another time, Yahweh tries to determine a proper course of action to destroy a hated king. In this account, the reader is given access to a debate in the divine council (1 Kgs. 22:19–22). The book of Deuteronomy gives a second picture of the divine council. Yahweh is a subordinate member of the council; another god, known as "El" or "Elyon," is the chief. It surprises me that later editors left the following passage intact:

> When the Most High [ʿelyôn] apportioned the nations,
>   when he divided humankind [běnê ʾādām],
> he fixed the boundaries of the peoples
>   according to the number of the gods [ʾelōhîm];
> the Lord's own portion was his people,
>   Jacob his allotted share.
>   (Deut. 32:8–9)

The chief god, ʿelyôn, assembles the ʾelōhîm and assigns various territories to them. The Israelite writer, with characteristic nationalism, declares that Elyon appointed the ʾelōhîm named Yahweh to the territory and the people known as Jacob, or Israel.[2] Note the disparity between these two aforementioned pictures of the divine council. In the earlier examples (Genesis, Job, 1 Kings), Yahweh appears as the head and ruler of the council. In Deuteronomy however, Yahweh is subordinate to ʿelyôn. How may we account for this change in the leadership of the council?

Traces of this story lie scattered throughout the Hebrew Bible. Enough remains to piece together a narrative. In Genesis 6, for example, the běnê haʾelōhîm (ʾelōhîm beings) sleep with the daughters of ʾādām. This action destabilizes the human community and brings on the flood. I suspect that behind this story is a longer and more complex tale. Two Hebrew prophets, condemning foreign kings, also borrow from this mythic narrative. Isaiah describes his king thusly:

> O Day Star, son of Dawn!
> How you are cut down to the ground,
>   you who laid the nations low!
> . . . .

---

2. It is nearly impossible to read this passage as if ʿelyôn and Yahweh are the same god, although many have tried. See J. Day 2000, 171, who identifies Elyon with both El and Baal.

But you are brought down to Sheol,
   to the depths of the Pit.
                    (Isa. 14:12, 15)

And Ezekiel says to a different king, over a century later:

Because your heart is proud
   and you have said, "I am a god [*ʾēl*]";
I sit in the seat of the gods [*ʾelōhîm*],
. . . .
They shall thrust you down to the Pit,
   and you shall die a violent death.
                    (Ezek. 28:2, 8)

Prophecies to proud kings begin to sound like ancient myths, which are stories of the gods. The psalmist declares that these kings will suffer the same fate as what happened to the *ʾelōhîm* in the Hebrew myth. Neither prophet tells the full details of the myth; they only refer to it. The fullest account of Yahweh's rise to prominence in the divine council and the demotion of the gods, their fall from power, however, is found in Psalms 58 and 82.

English translations of Psalms 58 and 82 have made a mess of them. In the following citations, whenever there is a divine name, I therefore give the Hebrew for these terms, and then proceed to discuss their meanings:

Psalm 58
   Truly, O *ʾēlem*, you pronounce judgment fairly. You judge the human realm according to just principles. (But in your heart you spread wickedness.) (vv. 1–2)
   There is [however an] *ʾelōhîm* who judges in the world. (v. 11)

Psalm 82
   ʾElōhîm arises in the congregation of *ʾēl*. In the midst of the *ʾelōhîm* he judges. (v. 1)
   I have said, "You are *ʾelōhîm*, and all of you are *ʿelyôn*'s children. Yet you shall die like mortals [*ʾādām*]. And like the other princes you shall fall. Arise, *ʾelōhîm*, judge the world; because [now] you own all the nations. (vv. 6–7)

In Psalm 58, the challenge to the *ʾēlem* immediately blends into a general condemnation of the wicked. We might identify "the wicked" as the

ʾēlem themselves, or their evil spawn. In Psalm 82, the general address is to the ʾelōhîm, the congregation of El (ʿădat-ʾēl), and the ʾelōhîm beings (bēnê ʾelōhîm). These three I regard as the same group.

El convenes a meeting of the gods. Yahweh is not the director and chairman of the board, but instead attends the meeting as a member. The mysterious god ʾēl lurks in the background as the absent father.[3] But the gods of the other nations prove unworthy of their great power and responsibility; they have not been serving as the protectors of their domain, nor have they promoted justice in their client states. Yahweh accuses them in the public forum and pronounces them dead.[4] This is a rare but not unheard of fate for divine beings.[5] They will die like mortals, Yahweh says, cast down to the depths.[6] Yahweh will assume all their responsibilities. Psalm 82 concludes with the hope that Yahweh (now in charge) will bring justice to the world. The poem then becomes an etiology that explains why Israelites worship Yahweh alone.[7]

In the first line of Psalm 82, the term ʾelōhîm is used in two entirely different ways. I will call the first usage ʾelōhîm 1: "ʾElōhîm arises in the

---

3. I agree with Smith's claim that the word ʾēl cannot be reduced to less than two meanings: the god El, and a generic god (M. S. Smith 1987, 136). He describes the confusion of using the word in two different ways: "El and Baal's relationship is fraught with tension and intrigue" (134). He associates El with the realm of the stars, while Baal rules over the lower sky, the place of storms. He goes on to say, "Common to all of these texts is a generational conflict that possibly reflects two (competing?) forms of divinity" (137). "Psalm 82 preserves a tradition that casts the god of Israel not in the role of the presiding god of the pantheon but as one of his sons" (156).

4. Smith says this about Yahweh's role in the council: "The author of Psalm 82 deposes the older theology, as Israel's deity is called to assume a new role as judge of the entire world. Yet at the same time, Psalm 82, like Deut. 32:8–9, *preserves the outlines of the older theology it is rejecting* [emphasis added]. From the perspective of this older theology, Yahweh did not belong to the top tier of the pantheon. Instead, in early Israel the god of Israel apparently belonged to the second tier of the pantheon; he was not the presider god, but one of his sons" (M. S. Smith 1987, 49).

5. "The notion of 'dead gods' is absent from the extant corpus of Israelite texts, with the exception of Psalm 82, which describes a divine council scene where Yahweh denounces the other gods as failing in their divine duties. Accordingly, Yahweh declares them to be 'dead'" (M. S. Smith, 1987, 100). Smith oscillates between two interpretations of "dead": (1) "dead" as having never existed, and (2) "dead" as having existed once but no longer.

6. There are two ways to understand the death of the gods in Psalm 82: (1) A universe where gods can die is a polytheistic universe, or (2) when the psalm says, "the gods will die," it is a poetic/mythological way to say that the gods never existed.

7. "The judgment announced is extreme. The gods are cast down from the heavenly sphere of life to the world of death. As unfaithful 'high officials' (sharim) are banished from court by a king, so the powers are driven away" (Kraus 1966, 157).

congregation of El" (*baʿădat-ʾēl*). So Yahweh occupies the central place for two reasons. First, he stands up as accuser and perhaps judge over the lesser gods. Second, by an act of extreme banishment, Yahweh seems to remain as the only god left. In the second part of the line, the poet introduces us to ʾ*elōhîm* 2: "In the midst of the ʾ*elōhîm* [2], he [presumably ʾ*elōhîm* 1] judges."

ʾ*Elōhîm* 1 (who is Yahweh, the god of Israel) and ʾ*elōhîm* 2 (the collection of lesser gods) are together meeting in the ʿ*ădat-ʾēl*, the congregation of ʾ*ēl*. Commonly, the first ʾ*elōhîm* (in agreement with the verb) is translated "God," while the second, which has no indication of number, is translated "gods." Both of the ʾ*elōhîm*s are subjects of ʾ*ēl*, part of his congregation (Handy 1990, 53). ʾ*Elōhîm* 1 (Yahweh) serves as accusing witness/attorney,[8] while a more powerful god, ʾ*ēl*, is the one to judge. Yahweh is also a member of the ʾ*elōhîm* 2, here understood as an aggregate of little gods. The NRSV translates the two occurrences of ʾ*elōhîm* differently. For the first it uses "God," because it occurs with a singular verb: "God has taken his place." In the second occurrence the NRSV reads "gods," because otherwise it does not make sense.

The NRSV treats this confusion as an oversight, or as a case of looseness in the language. It is as if the poet did not realize that he was using the same word in two places. Another explanation could be that the poet *deliberately subverted* these terms for God by placing them so ambiguously.[9] Wouldn't the poet have been perfectly capable of finding a less ambiguous word pair than ʾ*elōhîm* and ʾ*elōhîm*?

Some have suggested that the first ʾ*elōhîm* originally read *Yahweh* but was replaced by an Elohist editor, one of the Israelite writers whom scholars believe preferred to refer to God by the designation ʾ*elōhîm*. This theoretical Elohist editor was too dim-headed to notice that he had created an enormous obstacle to people understanding this poem (Kraus 1966, 154).

I think a much more likely explanation is that the author intended this confusion—that the author meant to communicate an idea by this odd usage. This psalm is a midway point between polytheism and monotheism, expressing ambiguity toward both and sharing characteristics with both (Kraus 1966, 155). Thus, there are two ʾ*elōhîm*s.

---

8. In the book of Job, the Satan serves a similar role. See Penchansky 1989.

9. Kselman notes that this psalm represents a "theological midpoint between Israel's early faith, in which the 'other gods' were real, but subordinate to Yahweh (Deut 4:19) and Israel's later monotheism" (1990, 540).

Psalm 82 pitches for monotheism. But if a committed monotheist, the psalmist employed an exceedingly strange way to advocate this religious idea. Usually when people argue for Yahweh's exclusive claims, they assume that the one supreme God has always held that position. There was never a time when Yahweh shared his classification "god" with others. However, Psalm 82 argues for monotheism by saying that Yahweh is the only god left, the best of the lot. It is a *chronological monotheism* that says that there is only one god now, although it has not always been so. Yahweh defeated the other gods in a divine law court, and now is the only god left standing. Therefore, other gods must have existed in the past. What these psalms suggest is that the *universe* went from polytheism to monotheism.[10] The other gods are real, though failed, divinities.

These two psalms seem to draw from a common narrative. These are some of their similarities:

> They both refer to divine beings other than the one Israelite God (Ps. 58: *ʾēlem*; Ps. 82: *ʾelōhîm*, *ʿădat-ʾēl*, and *běnê ʿelyôn*).
> They both seem to associate these terms with those whose responsibility it is to judge.
> In both, the one God (called *ʾelōhîm* in Ps. 82, *Yahweh* and *ʾelōhîm* in Ps. 58) judges the other divine beings.
> They both discuss two other groups of people: the wicked and the righteous.

The following are some significant differences:

> Psalm 82 has a plea for justice; Psalm 58 does not.
> Psalm 58 does not mention the poor.
> Psalm 58 asks God for just punishment of the wicked. Psalm 82 gives a divine pronouncement of judgment upon *ʾelōhîm*.

As these psalms have passed through more traditionally monotheistic communities, their meaning has been changed. John 10:34 is the earliest witness to this change in interpretation. Jesus claims to be one with the Father, as God's unique son. The people seek to stone him because "you,

10. Wright observes that the references to gods are not "mere" metaphors: "I find it difficult to regard these references as mere metaphors or as accommodating modes of speech. The actual existence of the other gods is here assumed." He goes on to argue against a polytheistic context for the psalm. The point is that they are without independent existence; they are responsible to the head of the council, Yahweh (Wright 1957, 35–36).

though only a human being, are making yourself God" (10:33). Jesus cites Psalm 82: "Is it not written in your law, 'I said, you are gods'?" He then offers the following interpretation: "If those to whom the word of God came were called 'gods' . . . can you say . . . [that I am] blaspheming because I said, 'I am God's son'?" He argues that the word "god" can in certain circumstances be applied to beings other than God himself (Emerton 1960, 332). Jesus, along with many Jewish interpreters, regarded the ʾelōhîm in Psalm 82 as human, Israelite judges whom God sentences because they failed to provide justice. This rabbinic interpretation of the word ʾelōhîm and of the psalm as a whole is, however, entirely too forced (Wright 1957, 31). The later editors of these texts had to develop reading strategies that harmonized them with their monotheistic ideas.

One cannot, however, divide up Israel's history so neatly into early polytheism and later monotheism. Rather, both beliefs coexisted and cross-pollinated throughout Israel's history. As Wright notes:

> [It is not] possible to portray a development in the Old Testament comprehension of the assembly from henotheism to monotheism. In fact, if one were forced to argue the question, he might maintain that the development is the opposite direction, since the assembly undeniably became more complex during the course of time. (Wright 1957, 37)

The divine council is not a vestige of an earlier Israelite religion but rather appears in literature throughout Israel's history.

There is a central tension at the heart of these psalms. Although they speak for universal devotion to Yahweh,[11] they create vivid renderings of these beings they profess not to believe in. Although these texts have been read monotheistically for thousands of years, such an interpretation has always been an ill fit. These psalms view the world in a different manner, barely mediated by later monotheistic ideas. They provide a model of how multiple and complex views of the divine might coexist within a single text, and by implication, how they have coexisted within the traditions stemming from the Hebrew Bible.

The presence of this myth in Israel tells us that ancient Israelite monotheism was complex and that the old monotheists had to account for the presence of polytheistic ideas in their canon. These other gods represented

---

11. "Rise up, O God, judge the earth; for all the nations belong to you!" (Ps. 82:8); "Surely there is a God who judges on earth" (Ps. 58:11).

a range of religious options that remained available to the Israelites throughout their long and turbulent history. The myth of a divine council coup, curiously and ambiguously both assumes a polytheistic universe (a council of gods ruled by a ruling god) and speaks of the death of polytheism—the demotion and death of all the gods except one. It therefore lies in the middle between these two religious ideas, polytheism and monotheism.

This myth of a fall from heaven might have served as an etiology to answer the questions "Why do we worship only Yahweh? What is the relationship of Yahweh to the other gods?" The answer would be, "Yahweh is the supreme God, and the other gods, whatever they once were, are irrelevant now." So this could be the story of how (and why) Israel worships a single god. But there are certain elements in the story, and certain absences, that suggest a more complex advocacy contained within these poems.

Psalm 82 allows for the possibility of there being other gods on the scene along with Yahweh. Yahweh has now condemned these other gods to death. But where gods existed before, they could exist again. Second Isaiah goes much further than that in his condemnation of polytheism. He represents another monotheist response to polytheism.

Chapter 5

Anti-Idol Polemic

An Attack on the Gods of Israel

O ne strategy used to overturn belief in other gods is satire, an attempt to poke fun at or ridicule the practices of polytheism. The prophet Jeremiah called idols (*pesel*; plural, *peselîm*) "scarecrows in a cucumber field" (10:5), because both scarecrows and idols are shaped like humans but cannot move or talk. He places them in a cucumber patch because that makes these figures seem ridiculous. The *peselîm* consist of carved or molded objects that represent the divine. They receive worship, sacrifice, and devotion.

Both Ezekiel and Jeremiah refer to Yahweh's rivals as "shit gods,"[1] and the narrator in Genesis portrays Rachel sitting on the concealed *teraphîm* (family gods?) while menstruating. These passages emphasize the helplessness of these gods, and their defilement. We find this motif employed numerous times in the Hebrew Bible. Second Isaiah employs it to great effect.

Most scholars affirm that an anonymous author (which they subsequently named Second Isaiah) wrote chapters 40–55 of the book of Isaiah some time toward the end of the Babylonian exile. Some decades earlier the Babylonian emperor had captured Jerusalem and forcibly moved the elite of the city, both religious and political leaders, and forced them to serve the empire as clerks in the city of Babylon.

Second Isaiah was written for this exilic community at the moment it faced the possibility of returning to its ancestral homeland. Nestled within

---

1. See Jer. 50:2 and Ezek. 22:3–4. This is what Edward Curtis says about "shit gods": "Images were called *gilulim*. . . . Irrespective of etymology, it appears that the negative and derogatory associations of the word comes from its similarity to the words *gel* and *galal*, both of which mean 'dung.' Thus the idols are referred to as 'dung pellets'" (Curtis 1992, 378).

Second Isaiah's message to these now hopeful exiles is a series of satiric poems that make fun of idol worshipers, making their religious beliefs and practices look ridiculous.

Second Isaiah does not attack the gods. Rather, he strikes at what he believes is polytheism's weakest point—that religious people represent their gods by statues and physical objects. For Second Isaiah, the *pesel* is the thing. It represents nothing outside of itself, but must be judged by what the statue itself (the object) can do. Idols, he might have said along with Jeremiah, are nothing more than scarecrows.

Second Isaiah's first point is that because human beings fashioned these idols they have less status and power than the humans who formed them. Idols cannot move but have to be carried about. *They cannot act to help:* Second Isaiah states, "These things you carry [the idols] are loaded as burdens on weary animals" (46:1). *They cannot understand:* "They do not know, nor do they comprehend; for their eyes are shut, so that they cannot see, and their minds as well, so that they cannot understand" (44:18). *They are subject to rot:* "As a gift one chooses mulberry wood—wood that will not rot" (40:20). *They are subject to toppling:* "One . . . seeks out a skilled artisan to set up an image that will not topple" (40:20) "they fasten it with nails so that it cannot be moved" (41:7).

In making his second argument, Second Isaiah points out that the craftsperson made the idol from profane sources:

> Half of it [the harvested wood] he burns in the fire; over this half he roasts meat, eats it and is satisfied. He also warms himself and says, "Ah, I am warm, I can feel the fire!" The rest of it he makes into a god, his idol, bows down to it and worships it; he prays to it and says, "Save me, for you are my god!" . . . No one considers, nor is there knowledge or discernment to say, "Half of it I burned in the fire; I also baked bread on its coals, I roasted meat and have eaten. Now shall I make the rest of it an abomination?" (44:16–19)

Why is it bad that the same wood is used for two different purposes, one as fuel for a cooking fire, the other as raw material to carve a *pesel*? Apparently, the author regarded meal cooking as a nonreligious act, and so the wood used in a cooking fire was tainted. If a sacred object were to have contact with a nonsacred object, the sacred object would become defiled. The same wood connects the two activities, cooking and idol worship. The author links the two behaviors. The idol cannot make the meal sacred, but rather the meal renders the idol unholy.

Second Isaiah's third point is that the production of an idol involves a technically demanding process. He implies that this high degree of human involvement precludes divine presence: "The ironsmith fashions it and works it over the coals, shaping it with hammers, and forging it with his strong arm. . . . The carpenter stretches a line, marks it out with a stylus, fashions it with planes, and marks it with a compass" (44:12–13). The artisans require a highly technical process to produce *pesêlîm*. The author indicates a deep knowledge of the processes of idol production, and this gives a sense of reality to the poem. Second Isaiah argues that the idols were not born as gods, but rather were manufactured. They did not originate supernaturally and so, by implication, are not worthy to be called gods.

Second Isaiah makes the worship of *pesêlîm* look silly. According to him, it cannot work, and does not do any good:[2] "He feeds on ashes; a deluded mind has led him astray, and he cannot save himself or say, 'Is not this thing in my right hand a fraud?'" (44:20). "All who make idols are nothing, and the things they delight in do not profit" (44:9). Moreover, worshiping *pesêlîm* brings shame and dishonor: "They shall all be put to shame" (44:11).[3]

Contrary to Second Isaiah, idol worshipers have almost always believed that their gods are more than a carved piece of wood or molded metal. For them, the *pesel* provides access to the god. It connects the worship to the deity and serves as a means to communicate, and as a reminder, a visual cue, and a focal point. It exemplifies a form of sympathetic magic that links the physical and spiritual realm; whatever the worshiper does for the idol on earth correspondingly accrues to the god in heaven (the "actual" god). Therefore, the god in heaven receives offerings that the devotee bestows upon the idol.

The *pesel*, understood as a physical object, serves as a portal to the god's abode. Therefore, Second Isaiah's description of the nature and belief of paganism is profoundly inaccurate. How did he come to such a serious error? Kaufmann suggests that the prophet was so naive regarding the actual beliefs of the pagans that he was capable of making such a grievous error (1960, 20). Second Isaiah distorted polytheistic worship because he had no exposure to true idol worship. Kaufmann assumes that Israelite monotheistic ideology developed in isolation from the surrounding cultures.

---

2. Goldingay observes, "The hyperbole, the irony, the ridicule, and the satire imply that only a fool would dispute the matter under discussion" (1997, 227).

3. It is no accident that the second commandment, against the creation of images, is not mentioned here. The warrant in Second Isaiah is not divine law but rather ridicule and the assertion of the obvious.

I suggest, contrariwise, that the prophet misrepresented the *pesĕlîm* to deliberately distort how his captors worshiped. Clearly, Second Isaiah was aware of pagan practice. He lived, after all, in Babylon, and showed a detailed understanding of the technical aspects of idol production. How then did this distortion serve Isaiah's community?[4]

The returning exiles were only one of many religious groups found among the Jewish communities in the postexilic period. Second Isaiah's anti-idol polemic served the needs of *his* community at the expense of other competing communities. Second Isaiah brought this message to the returning exiles that Yahweh was the only God and that all the other gods were blocks of wood. These returning exiles sought to legitimate their claims to the land by making illegitimate the claims of others.

Second Isaiah wrote to delegitimate the claims of others. These others were those "Israelites" who had stayed in Palestine during the Babylonian exile. They consisted mostly of the lower classes and had continued their polytheistic practices. They were, however, Yahwists and they obeyed the first commandment. They had no other gods when they worshiped in Yahweh's presence. Apparently, they transgressed the second commandment, having images of their gods (as did the ancestors of Israel and many of the Israelite and Judean kings). Second Isaiah sought to undermine their legitimacy by mocking their habits of worship. Additionally, he mocked those who in their religious practice sought to imitate their captors.

The returning exiles made arguments from history and theology. From a historical perspective, they claimed, "We are the only true, the only pure Israelites." They argued theologically, "We maintain the true, authentic beliefs of our forebears." However, the other people with claim to the land were probably idol worshipers. Although the more obvious target of Second Isaiah's parody would be his Babylonian hosts, likely the prophet indirectly sought to delegitimate the claims of these poorer Judean people, those who had stayed in Palestine. His description of the *pesel*-maker is a deliberate distortion of the way that *pesĕlîm* truly functioned, a distortion for purposes of attacking an alternative religious/theological perspective. The way that Israelites had always worshiped the gods now has been declared invalid. Second Isaiah attacks the contemporary representatives of those beliefs (the Israelites who had not been taken to Babylon) by accusing them of believing a foolish, foreign religion.

---

4. The following discussion draws heavily on these parts of the following works: Berquist 2000, 32–34; Oded 1977, 484–88; Gottwald 1992, 43–57.

The Palestinian natives called Samaritans in postexilic writings opposed the return of the exiles. The Bible attacks the religious pedigree of the Samaritans and regards them as a foreign nation with no previous connection with the returning exiles. By the time of the New Testament, Samaria had become a symbol of degraded behavior. However, we need not accept at face value Second Isaiah's depiction of these other communities. Second Isaiah seeks to erase these indigenous people so that his community might rightfully displace and replace them. But these first settlers had prior claim to the land that both groups wanted. Therefore, Second Isaiah accuses these others of being dregs and half-breeds.[5]

Second Isaiah represented the exiles, those that had been the leaders and ruling elite in Israel before the Babylonians conquered them.[6] It was to his group's advantage to prove that others who claimed historical connection to Israel were imposters; their claim to the land was false because their worship was tainted.[7] The Israelites/Judeans who did not go into exile continued to worship gods other than Yahweh, and continued to use idols. Such activity is entirely consistent with the archaeological and textual evidence of earlier Israelite civilization.

Isaiah's description is wrong because he did not describe actual pagan theology. The returning exiles wanted to create an ideological space in which to justify their encroachment upon territory that had been occupied by native Judeans for fifty years. They tell a story of how the land was empty all this time, and how the few inhabitants, the dregs, polluted themselves with foreign practices and lost any legitimate claim on the land as well as any claim on the names "Israel," "Judah," or "Jew."

It is likely that Second Isaiah's anti-idol polemic is directed against this group. Scholars commonly locate Second Isaiah during the waning days of the exile. There was much political activity during this time, related to the declining fortunes and influences of Babylon and the rise of Persia.

5. These particular anti-image polemics are directed against those who had stayed in Palestine during the exile, whose religion might have been truer to the original form of Israelite religion than what the displaced Judeans had proposed. The Judeans subsequently won, and succeeded in defining the whole. However, as Eagleton says (quoted by Gottwald), "The text exists in the 'hollow' it has scooped out between itself and history" (Gottwald 1992, 43).

6. Gottwald 1992, 43: "The text of Isaiah 40–55 is shown to be a weapon of struggle to preserve the socio-cultural identity and political fixture of a former Judahite."

7. Carroll notes with some bitterness that the myth of the occupied land reflects the ideology of a polluting force identified with the people(s) of the land and underwrites the antiassimilationist policies of the temple community. The holy community living in the holy city in the holy land must keep itself separate from all outsiders (the peoples of the land) so as not to endanger itself by further exposure to Yahweh's wrath against such pollutant forces (1992, 91).

Second Isaiah's concerns were not purely religious, but had a strong political component. The returning exiles were about eradicate an entire people through subjugation, erasing them by declaring them different and inferior. They sought to displace a group from an identifiably poorer class, but one that nevertheless had inherited the land.[8]

Another reason to question Second Isaiah's position is that he applies his principles inconsistently. Israel too created physical objects as a means to gain access to God. The problem with the *peselîm* is a wider problem also present in Israel, and perhaps is a structural problem of all religions that try to embrace the goodness of the material world. The writer's dirty little secret is that Yahweh too is represented through descriptive words (spoken by Second Isaiah himself) and through sacred objects, most notably the ark of the covenant.

The ark consisted of a wooden box overlaid with gold, and two golden statues, sphinxlike cherubim, reached their wings across the golden slab on top. The Israelites left an empty space between the cherubim as a profound and multilayered symbol of how physical space might represent divine presence. But that empty space is Yahweh as much as a *pesel* represents its god. We do not know of an actual carved image of Yahweh in Israel's official cult, but that does not significantly alter the ancient theology as much as is usually imagined. Yahweh is still localized, still associated with some expression of materiality, still inhabiting human-fashioned space.

The Israelites described Yahweh using terms from the human body. How then can Second Isaiah mock the idol worshipers for their physical renderings of the divine? For instance, Second Isaiah speaks concerning Yahweh:

> Who has measured the waters in the hollow of his hand
>   and marked off the heavens with a span,
>   enclosed the dust of the earth in a measure?
>
> (40:12)

It has been said before: The winners write history. I want to add to this bromide: The winners are not always the best of the lot. The complexities and flaws in the arguments of even the pro-monotheists suggest that

---

8. Goldingay (1997, 237) argues that the Judean exiles were a small elite and were not even unified among themselves about Second Isaiah's points: "A community once used to power and significance, they were people who now found themselves insignificant and powerless." Cf. Carroll 1992, 79, 90; Widengren (1977, 511–12).

in ancient Israel there always existed active polytheists, not only as outlaws and foreigners. A nearly thoroughgoing monotheism introduced by Second Isaiah and his minions was in fact the innovation, the new and radical idea. Israel mostly understood Yahweh as one god among many, and the radical monotheists sought to eradicate that.

Part 2

The Goddesses of Ancient Israel

W hen I began to write this book, I expected to find that Yahweh and each of the goddesses mentioned in the Bible formed a couple. I expected that at various times Yahweh would have chosen this or that female deity as his consort or wife. Instead I found that two of these goddesses (Hokmah and Lady Zion) were Yahweh's *daughters*, and the only evidence that Yahweh had a wife is found outside the ancient text, in ancient inscriptions dug up in the nineteenth and twentieth centuries.

The first chapter of Genesis describes humans as made in the image of God. The writer carefully specifies through parallel writing that the image of God is male *and* female:

> So God created humankind in his image,
>   in the image of God he created them;
>   male and female he created them.

By making parallel the terms "image of God" and "male and female," the writer stressed that the God of whom he spoke had the qualities of both maleness and femaleness. Ordinarily, gods in the ancient Near East were either male or female, and both were needed to bring life and fertility to the world. They achieved this through their sexual union. But the writer of Genesis 1 insists that God needed no consort because he possessed the qualities of both male and female, so in a sense, he could self-fertilize and bring life into the world with no help from a wife.

The Israelites, at least as portrayed in the Bible, were remarkably skittish about the sexuality of their national god, Yahweh. This means they never spoke of Yahweh's sexual organs, unlike the stories of other West Semitic gods (see Eilberg-Schwartz 1994, especially chapter 3) and they never spoke of Yahweh as being with a goddess. Asherah (by inference in the Bible, and from archaeological discoveries) is the exception that proves the rule.

Chapter 6

Hokmah and the Ideology of Monotheism

My thesis for this book is that there exist in the Bible divine forces other than Yahweh.[1] An obvious test case for this thesis is Hokmah, the personification of wisdom that first appears in Proverbs.[2] I have long been attracted to this divine figure, who invites young men back to her house to eat, teaching them the proper manner in which to live their lives. I wonder along with Roland Murphy, "Just who is she, and what is she up to?" (Murphy 1998, 53). I ask further: What is she doing in this monotheistic document, the Hebrew canon, if monotheism won out?

Hokmah appears in fragments throughout the first ten chapters of Proverbs, and also in the deuterocanon. She continues to show up in both rabbinic and early Christian writings. When we take these fragments together, there emerges a compelling unified biography of her, which recounts her birth and early childhood, her teaching career, her relationship with her students, and how she competes with the so-called Strange Woman for disciples and lovers.

In Proverbs, she first appears on the street corner, urging young men to listen to her (Prov. 1:20–33). She later invites them to her house for a feast (9:1–11).[3] In Proverbs 8, Hokmah declares herself, discloses herself,

---

1. An earlier version of this chapter was published in Adam 2001, 81–92.

2. The feminine word *ḥokmah* is the Hebrew word for wisdom. When it refers to a person, "Lady Wisdom" might be the best rendering.

3. The "house" might be a temple with pillars, which would suggest Hokmah as a goddess with her own cult. I am grateful to my colleague Professor Corrine Carvalho for this insight.

and gives her history.[4] She invites the foolish to follow her.[5] She gives life and counsel to kings.

I will focus upon the poem recited by Hokmah in Proverbs 8:22–31. It provides the fullest and most vivid depiction of her, how she was born, her relationship with Yahweh, and her delight in humanity. Much of the poem speaks of how Hokmah instructs the wise in the courts of the powerful. However, in the midst of this poem of self-praise, Hokmah begins to speak of the cosmic realm. From the world of kings and simpletons we move into a world of primal beginnings, peopled by the gods and the sacred elements of mythic geography, the deep (*těhōm*), the mountains, the fountains, the heavens, and so on. All these, whether animate or inanimate, are infused with power in this creative moment, the beginning of the universe. This poem, I argue, portrays Hokmah as an Israelite goddess.

Hokmah in Proverbs 8:22–31

How does the author of Proverbs understand Hokmah? As I said, Hokmah inhabits most fully the passage 8:22–31 in Proverbs. This is the New Revised Standard Version with some of my own modifications:

> Yahweh acquired [NRSV, "created"] me at the beginning of his work,
>   the first of his acts of long ago.
> Ages ago I was poured out [NRSV, "set up"],
>   at the first, before the beginning of the earth.
> When there were no depths I was brought forth,
> . . . .
> When he marked out the foundations of the earth,
>   then I was beside him, like an *ʾāmôn;* [NRSV, "a master worker"];
> and I was a daily delight,
>   Always playing right in front of him [NRSV, "rejoicing before him
>   always"],
> playing in his inhabited world
>   and delighting in the human race.

4. Lang observes, "Proverbs 8 is one of the most developed mythological texts of the Bible, reminiscent of the kind of discourse characteristic of the Homeric Hymns" (1999, 902).

5. She does this in direct competition with another woman, the Strange Woman, or the Foreign Woman, who also invites young men to her house (Prov. 2:16–19; 5:3–14). See also references to "the evil woman" (6:24–35; 7:6–23) and "the foolish woman" (9:13) (Camp 1987, 71–72).

I will organize my initial thoughts on this text around four different aspects of Hokmah found in the poem:

1. The time of her birth and activity
2. The circumstances of her birth
3. Her activity after birth, her playing
4. The translation of the word *ʾāmôn*

"Once Upon a Time": Hokmah in Her Temporal Setting

In English, many fairy tales introduce their narratives with "once upon a time." This is a literary cue whereby a difference is created between the time of the story and the time of the reader. By saying "once upon a time," the storyteller creates a qualitative, not a quantitative distinction. This is a time when things happen differently. The reader cannot trace an unbroken temporal line from "once upon a time" to her own. The two times exist as two different universes.

Hokmah exists in this separate universe, which we might here call the cosmic realm. This is indicated by the use of Hebrew cues that function similarly to what "once upon a time" means in English. The poet describes Hokmah's time as *mēʾāz*—literally, "from then." The line then may be translated, "I was the first of his acts *of long ago*" (8:22), or "once upon a time." The poet deepens this impression by use of the word *mēʿôlām* in the next verse, translated *"Ages ago* I was poured out"; one might also say, "in days of old." Mythic time, inhabited by gods and primal objects, is this time of origins, and this is where we find Hokmah.

In the poem, Hokmah shares the stage with *tĕhôm*, translated "the depths," meaning "the primal waters," perhaps the uncreated raw stuff of the universe. Hokmah declares, "When there was no *tĕhôm* I was brought forth." She also precedes the mountains, the heavens, and the fountains, objects that constitute a veritable Jungian paradise of archetypes. Hokmah claims priority over all these others. She says, for instance, "Before the mountains had been shaped, before the hills . . . I was there." Also, she witnessed the creation of all these "when he established the fountains of the deep . . . then I was beside him [Yahweh]."

Hokmah's Birth

The poet employs three different terms that describe Hokmah's origin. They are *qānāh*, "Yahweh *acquired* me" (v. 22); *nisaktî* "I was *poured out*" (v. 23); and *ḥôlāltî*, "I was *brought forth*" (v. 24). *Qānāh* might be defined as "create,"[6] or it could refer to Hokmah's birth, as when Eve named her first son Cain because she had "acquired" from Yahweh a son.[7]

The NRSV translates *nisaktî* as "set up," but this term might refer to creation by pouring, a ceramic process whereby the materials are poured into a mold. In the case of Hokmah, we might understand the mold as the divine womb. Compare this to Genesis 2 when Yahweh "formed" the first man as a potter shapes a pot. Lang's alternative interpretation of the word bears repeating. He suggests that *nisaktî* refers to an "outpouring of generative semen" (Lang 1986, 63).[8]

The final word, *ḥôlāltî* (from the root *ḥûl* or *ḥîl*), refers to the writhing motions of a woman in childbirth:[9] "When there were no depths I was brought forth [*ḥôlāltî*] . . . before the hills, I was brought forth" (Prov. 8:24–25). The verses thereby indicate that Yahweh is a divine parent, both father and mother. This would not be the only time such a thing has happened. There are other accounts in ancient mythology where a male god births deities without benefit of a corresponding female god. Greek mythology, for instance, speaks of Athena, born from Zeus's head. In the Bible itself, Eve came from Adam's body. And in a later apocryphal book, Sirach, the writer has Hokmah say, "I came forth from the mouth of the Most High, / and covered the earth like a mist" (24:3).[10]

6. Landes notes regarding the word *qānānî*, "The meaning 'to beget, produce, create,' would seem to be earlier than the much more common 'to buy, acquire, possess'" (1974, 281). Dahood also translates this as "begot." Whybray concurs, saying, "Although there is only one word that strictly means sexual birth in the passage . . . the other two verbs have alternative meanings that include sexual birth. *q-n-h* is used in some places to mean 'give birth,' as when Eve says she has 'gotten' a child from the Lord. And 'set up' (*nāsāk*) can mean to have been 'woven' together in the womb" (1994, 131) See also Ringgren 1947, 101–2.

7. But see P. Davies 1995, 92, where he reads *qanah* in both this and the Genesis passage as "create." Eve, according to Davies, is claiming an action of deity, and is not using birthing language. (I am grateful to my colleague Corrine Carvalho for directing me to this book).

8. Landes (1974, 281) states that "the verb *nisaktî*, if the Masoretic pointing is correct, refers to a creation by 'outpouring,' apparently a very archaic idea in the ancient Near East, though used only here in that sense in the Old Testament." Lang agrees (1986, 63)

9. Lang observes, "She is not the product of the artisan's skill, nor has she been conquered in battle to be made part of the ordered world. Rather, she has been *born* or brought forth by birth. Wisdom says of herself, 'I was born [*ḥôlāltî*],' an expression used to refer to human birth" (1986, 63).

10. Lang observes, "Within religious history there are several gods without mothers, and Wisdom may belong to these. . . . Similarly, the Egyptian god Thoth . . . sprang from the head of Seth. Such paradoxical phenomena are labeled 'male pregnancy' and 'male birth,' ideas not entirely foreign to the Bible" (1986, 64–65).

Rather than portraying Hokmah as a mother-goddess like the Canaanite goddess Asherah (to whom Hokmah has been compared), Yahweh himself becomes the birth parent (Day 2000, 67). Claudia Camp observes, "The process of Yahweh's conception, bearing and birth of Wisdom is here depicted without reservation" (Camp 1985, 84). Lang carries the birth imagery further than many:

> While the creation of the material world can be referred to in terms of craftsmanship and building activities[,] . . . Wisdom's creation must be spoken of in personal terms: Wisdom was "begotten [his translation of *qānāh*]," "fashioned [*nisaktî*]" (as in the womb), and eventually "born." Gods are not created as the world is created; they are begotten and born, not made [*ḥôlāltî*]. There is a qualitative difference between gods and the realm of the created. (Lang 1986, 77)

These three words, "set up," used one time, "poured out," used once, and "brought forth/birthed," used twice, give evidence that Hokmah was qualitatively different from all the other inhabitants of the new universe. She was Yahweh's child rather than Yahweh's creation.

Hokmah Plays

And I was a daily delight,
   always playing right in front of him,
playing in his inhabited world
   and delighting in the human race.
         (Prov. 8:30–31)

Hokmah plays, frolics, and rejoices. "To play before the head of household in this part of the world was to be part of the family. It speaks of deep intimacy" (Lang 1986, 78).

The *tĕhōm*, by contrast, is *inscribed*, the mountains are *shaped*, and the heavens are *established*. The fountains *abound* in water. These others function as things for Hokmah to admire. What a contrast with the two verbs that describe Hokmah's activity: She "plays" (from the verb *śḥq*), and she "delights" (*šaʿašʿîm*; from *sin-ayin-ayin*). She declares herself a "daily delight, always playing right in front of him."[11] Yahweh delights in her,

---

11. This is usually translated "daily *his* delight," but "his" is not in the Hebrew and is not required by the context.

and she in turn delights in the *běnê ʾādām* ("human race"). So Hokmah bridges in this word "delight" the human and the divine realms. She is deeply connected by delight to both God (Yahweh who admires Hokmah and delights in her) and humanity.[12]

The Hebrew term used for "play" can mean many different things: children's play, playing an instrument, jesting, or mocking. A related word that replaces the Hebrew letter *śîn* with the *ṣādê* sometimes refers to sexual play or fondling. Isaac thus fondles (*měṣaḥēq*) his wife" in Genesis 26:8 and the Israelites' play might imply sexual activity in Exodus 32:6: "The people sat down to eat and drink, and rose up to revel." "Revel" translates another form of the same Hebrew word. Because of the birth imagery and the "delight" words (which usually indicate a parent-child relationship), children's play best fits the context of Proverbs 8. The participants in the narrative delight in each other (Yahweh, Hokmah, and humanity). There is also play, which takes place both in the presence of Yahweh (or in one interpretation, "on his lap"; Gese 1981, 31) and in his inhabited world.

Play is carefree, full of pleasure and whimsy. As Camp observes, "No oppressive order, not even Yahweh's, is secure where children play, lovers meet, and life comes forth" (1987, 61). She goes on to say, "Play is a fundamentally liminal, deconstructive activity. For Wisdom, it takes place at the heart of the interaction between God and humans and thus at the heart of the theological endeavor" (61). Hokmah, playing, stands at the boundaries between childhood and adulthood, between fantasy/imagination and mundane reality, between chaos and order. She is serious but not solemn. The activity in which she engages is both frivolous and absolutely vital for human well-being.

I had originally expected that I would find that Hokmah served as Yahweh's female sexual companion in Proverbs 8. When I looked at the poem more closely, this did not seem to fit. Rather, Hokmah's erotic attachment is to humanity. The teacher commands the student to say of Hokmah, "You are my sister" (Prov. 7:4). In Hebrew idiom, this most commonly is a term of endearment. The writer urges the student, "Do not forsake her[;] . . . love her[;] . . . embrace her" (4:6–8), and finally we hear from Hokmah herself: "I love those who love me" (8:17).[13] In this way she

---

12. See also Jer. 31:20: "Is Ephraim my dear son? Is he the child I delight in?"

13. Her blandishments, however, are much subtler and less private than those of the Strange Woman.

"plays" with humanity. She relates to Yahweh, however, as a young daughter to her father.

Hokmah, the ʾĀmôn of Yahweh

Then I was beside him, like an ʾāmôn.

(Prov. 8:30)

The word ʾāmôn is central to an understanding of the poem, because it describes Hokmah's relationship to Yahweh. By use of the preposition ʾeṣel, translated "beside," this word provides the key link between Yahweh and Hokmah. First we have Yahweh creating the universe, while Hokmah, a little girl, plays at his side. Unfortunately, the word ʾāmôn remains indecipherable in the Masoretic Text.[14] Some of the Rabbis and the Septuagint read ʾāmôn as "master architect" or "builder." Other traditions translate it "nursling" or "child."[15] This wide disparity of early traditions suggests that by the first centuries of the Common Era, readers already had lost the meaning.

Interpreting the word as "nursling" or "little child" seems the best option. Language of birth and playing infer the presence of a child. In these verses Hokmah is born. She delights and plays. A "little child" does such

---

14. Concerning Jer. 52:15, Terrien writes, "Nebuzaradan the captain of the guard carried into exile some of the poorest of the people and the rest of the people who were left in the city, and the deserters who had defected to the king of Babylon, together with the rest of the artisans." The word translated "artisans" is haʾāmôn, which has been identified as a source for the word in Proverbs 8. However, this connection is controversial and according to Terrien serves as "an unreliable precedent" (Terrien 1981, 135; see also Fox 1969, 699). See also Num. 11:12; Ruth 4:16; Esth. 2:7; Isa. 49:23; Lam. 4:5 "[Translating it as 'workman'] would require the repointing of ʾāmôn to ʾāmûn, the passive participle qal of aman" (Whybray 1994, 136).

15. No final adjudication is possible; the meaning was likely lost early. These two most common interpretations have been joined by others. All require some emendation, and none has emerged as the clear leader. Lang 1986, 65, gives an overview of the five basic interpretations of ʾāmôn:

1. I was at his side as an *infant*
2. I was at his side as a *confidant*
3. I was at his side as a *master builder* (or architect). Murphy also takes this position because it represents the earliest witnesses.
4. I was at his side as a *counselor* (McKane 1970).
5. I was at the side of the master builder—that is, not the master builder herself. Only God is the master builder. Hokmah is at God's side while *he* builds. Dahood is one who has taken this position (1968, 513).

things. In Proverbs 8, Hokmah does not create or design the universe (although she does build a house with pillars), and so "master architect" would seem out of place.[16] The term remains ambiguous, and this adds to Hokmah's mystery and independence.[17] This interpretive knot, the intractability of the word *ʾāmôn*, is perhaps a key feature of the text. It creates an open symbol that different communities fill in different ways.

In sum, this poem depicts Hokmah as a female figure who claims divine origin in the mythic past. She began before anything else, and she began differently from anything else, before any of the primal objects. She plays and rejoices before Yahweh as he creates the world. We might say that Yahweh has created the world for his little child's entertainment, to give her delight and joy.

The Ancient Problem of Hokmah

Camp correctly observes that Hokmah engages in "a virtual usurpation of Yahweh's prerogatives, e.g., as giver of life and death (8:35–36); as the source of legitimate government (8:15–16); as the one to be sought after and called (1:28); as one who loves and is to be loved (8:17); and as the giver of security (1:33) and wealth (8:15–16)" (1985, 28).[18] As Scott puts it, "She speaks for herself and with her own authority, like a goddess" (1965, 39). Roland Murphy refers to Hokmah in this way: "There is no personification comparable to that of wisdom. Justice and peace may kiss (Ps. 85:11 [10]), and alcohol may be a rowdy (Prov. 20:1), but only wisdom is given a voice that resembles the Lord's (Prov. 8:35, 'whoever finds me finds life')" (1995, 222–23).

As significant portions of the Israelite community consolidated their loyalties and focused exclusively on Yahweh, the meaning of Hokmah had

16. Michael Fox observes, "Wisdom does not seem to directly affect the course of events. . . . Wisdom fills her role less by doing than by *being*" (Fox 1997, 629). He also says, "The emphasis on Wisdom's play in vv. 30–31 seems to be a deliberate refutation of the notion that Wisdom had an active productive role in the work of creation" (Fox 1996, 700).

17. Scott agrees: "From an early date there was much uncertainty about the vocalization and meaning of this important word" (1960, 215). Terrien observes, "The precise meaning of the notoriously difficult word *ʾāmôn* defies demonstration" (1981, 135). Bernhard Lang translates Proverbs 8:31, "I was beside him as an infant whom he (the Creator) has nursed" (1986, 66). Lang's choice of words might not be a translation, but rather a deliberate midrashic misreading. See Whybray (1994, 134), who says that *ʾāmôn* remains irreducible to one plain meaning. See also Scott (1965, 72), who emphasizes how "workman" requires serious emendation of the text.

18. Fontaine observes, "The unanswered question of this scholarly reconstruction is the manner in which Israelite sages would have borrowed material from traditions so roundly condemned elsewhere in the canon" (1988, 502). By "traditions" she means "goddess traditions."

to be rethought and retooled. Even though her presence might have embarrassed a staunch monotheist, authors kept on writing about her in the deuterocanon, in early Jewish writings, and in early Christianity. However, the changes they made in her reduced the threat she presented to God's primacy.

Note these three examples:

> "I came forth from the mouth of the Most High,
>   and covered the earth like a mist.
> I dwelt in the highest heavens,
>   and my throne was in a pillar of cloud.
> . . . .
> Then the Creator of all things gave me a command.
> . . . .
> He said, 'Make your dwelling in Jacob.'"
> . . . .
> All this is the book of the covenant of the Most High God,
>   the law that Moses commanded us
>   as an inheritance for the congregations of Jacob.
>   (Sir. 24:3–4, 8, 23; see also 1:1–10, 24:1–33)
>
> For she is a breath of the power of God,
> and a pure emanation of the glory of the Almighty.
> . . . .
> For she is a reflection of eternal light,
> a spotless mirror of the working of God,
> and an image of his goodness.
>   (Wis. 7:25–26; see also 7:7–14, 22–30)

> [He] gave her to his servant Jacob
>   and to Israel, whom he loved.
> Afterward she appeared on earth
>   and lived with humankind.
> She is the book of the commandments of God,
>   the law that endures forever.
>   (Bar. 3:36–4:1; see also 3:9–35)

They all expand on the description of Hokmah in Proverbs 8. They identify her as the creator of the world and the embodiment of torah, the way of life of the Jews.

In the rabbinical writings we find, "ʾāmôn', this is Torah. The Holy One Blessed Be He was looking into Torah, as he was creating the universe.

Therefore [we read]: And I was with him ʾāmôn.'"[19] These writings for the most part retreated from the compelling level of verisimilitude one finds in Proverbs 8. The later traditions treat Hokmah as an abstraction. Her audacious presence in the divine realm troubled later Jewish writers. They sought to mute her influence in order to give more presence and reality to the Supreme God. Her continuing existence, however, indicates that the Jewish writers in the early centuries of the Common Era were not beholden to the stricter understanding of God, which I have called radical monotheism.

Early Christians (in the New Testament up to the time of the Nicene Creed) clearly were aware of the Israelite/Jewish tradition of Hokmah. They lifted phrases and ideas from Proverbs 8 and the deuterocanon and used them to describe Christ. The writing concerning the divine origin of Hokmah and the intimate familial relationships she enjoyed with Yahweh were applied to the Son of God in the Christian tradition. Like Hokmah, he was the firstborn of creation.[20] From the deuterocanon, early Christians borrowed terms linked with Hokmah to assign Christ a role in creation. For instance, John 1:3 says, "All things came into being through him." In Colossians 1:15, the author writes that Christ is "the firstborn of all creation," and in Hebrews 1:2, we learn that through Christ, God created the world.[21] Scott claims that "the definition in the Nicene Creed, 'begotten not made,' may have rested in part on the birth metaphor in vss. 24–25 [of Proverbs]" (Scott 1965, 69–70).

In both Judaism and Christianity, Hokmah becomes a manifestation of one or another very important aspect of God, but she never completely loses her identity.[22] She becomes a kind of hypostatization, which was a way for those beginning in the early centuries before the Common Era to

19. Tanhuma, Berashit 5. I am indebted to Shoshana Brown for this and other rabbinic passages. See also in Sifre Debarim (chapter 37); and in Pes. 54a. From Brown, "We see in the above passages of Talmud and the midrashim that certain verses from Proverbs 8 were quite popular proof-texts for establishing the pre-existence of Torah."

20. See Murphy 1998, 281, and Scott 1960, 215.

21. Scott provides a concise summary of later occurrences of the Hokmah figure: "The Wisdom of Solomon speaks of 'Wisdom, the fashioner of all things' (7:22 EV), as 'an associate in His works' (8:4), and as 'fashioner of all that exists' (7:6); Philo (*de Sacerdot* 5) says that 'the universe was fabricated' through the agency of the Logos-Wisdom; the same thought appears in John 1:3, 'through him all things came to be'; in Col. 1:15–16, 'the first born of all creation, for in him all things were created'; and in Heb 1:2, 'through whom also he created the world.' The influence of Proverbs 8 on these passages, and consequently on later Christological doctrine, is evident" (1965, 69–70).

22. Philo associates Hokmah with *logos* and *sophia*.

speak about these other gods while maintaining the illusion of radical monotheism. I define "hypostasis" as a semi-independent manifestation of the one god.[23] These manifestations appear as separate personalities, but actually they represent an *aspect* of the one God. In ancient times, hypostasis was used to justify the importance of Hokmah. In modern times it has been used to diminish her importance.[24] Hokmah becomes in later writings a part of God, an emanation of the divine being. How could this happen? We might see that the independent god known as Hokmah comes under greater and greater influence from Yahweh, until the division between the two breaks down and they begin to share qualities. Aspects of Hokmah become a part of Yahweh and Hokmah comes to be regarded as a particular manifestation of Yahweh. A second understanding would see that as the Israelite God increases in power and remoteness, he spins off these safer and more manageable aspects of himself.

The ancient writers found Hokmah in Proverbs 8 troublesome, and so they wrote about her in such a way so that she gave less trouble. If the divine figure was more goddess than they were comfortable with, they reduced her independence by abstraction and hypostatization. She maintains, however, a surprising vibrancy even in these works, and that is why she continues.

The Modern Problem of Hokmah

As with the ancient world, for modern scholars Hokmah presents problems. The presence of an Israelite goddess in this literature does not fit in with the more traditional understanding that Israel began in a pagan context and later developed to monotheism. According to this way of understanding the development of Israelite belief, when Israel passed from paganism to monotheism, it thereby moved from inauthenticity to authenticity, from falsehood and illusion to reality. Hokmah threatens or

23. This is Lang's definition: "a being that emanates from a higher reality to which it owes its existence and force, but one which also enjoys a certain independence" (Lang 1999, 904). Camp uses Oesterly's definition: "a quasi-personification of certain attributes proper to God, [occupying] an intermediate position between personalities and abstract beings" (Camp 1985, 33–34).

24. But see M. S. Smith 1987, 102: "The avoidance of anthropomorphic imagery was by no means a general feature of Israelite religion after the Exile. While the tendency away from anthropomorphism marks priestly and Deuteronomistic traditions belonging to the eighth through the fifth centuries, later works belonging to the priestly traditions continued to transmit anthropomorphic imagery."

challenges this traditional understanding in two ways. First, Proverbs 1–10 is regarded as a late document (postexilic), so it could not represent some earlier, primitive form of Israelite religion.[25] There should be no goddess in a late, postexilic document, according to the traditional understanding.

Hokmah is too positive, too real, and too vibrant for the monotheistic sensibilities of modern commentators. Scholars therefore have to account for the late appearance of Hokmah at a time when it is assumed that the Israelites had supposedly expunged all traces of polytheism from their midst. How do we have a goddess figure in a text that most scholars regard as late? Two arguments emerged in the twentieth century as strategies to distance Hokmah from polytheistic beliefs and practices. In the first, Hokmah is a goddess, but not an *Israelite* goddess. In the second, Hokmah is characteristically Israelite, but she is not a goddess.

The first alternative claims Hokmah is a goddess but that she has no Israelite pedigree. What then is her origin? Scholars have offered three different explanations: (1) She remains as a vestige of Israel's ancient pagan past. (This is the historical argument.) (2) She is a foreign goddess imported into Israel and polluting its pristine monotheism, coming from Sumer, Egypt, Canaan, Babylon, or Greece. (This is a geographical argument.)[26] (3) Finally, there are those who say that Hokmah is part of popular worship and not part of the "official" religion. This is an argument based on class distinction. Only the common people believed in her, they say.[27]

Some approach the problem of Hokmah differently. They accept her Israelite pedigree but deny her divinity. For some, she is not a goddess or any kind of mythological personality, but rather a mere figure of speech. Carole Fontaine observes, "Woman Wisdom and Woman Stranger become 'mere' literary devices whose symbolic meaning becomes relatively

25. The dating of wisdom literature is difficult because it lacks standard cues. The assumption is made (with some merit) that wisdom tends to move from less complex to more complex, from shorter segments to longer, from practical concerns to philosophical/theological concerns, and from a tribal context to one more urban and centralized. On that basis, Proverbs 1–10 is late. See Lang 1986, 4, and Scott 1965, 39, for a different view.

26. See Kloppenborg 1982, 61. Camp observes, "In rather unabashed fashion, Wisdom takes over imagery associated with Ma'at, Astarte-Ishtar, Anat and royal goddesses, sharing some of these features with the strange woman" (Camp 1987, 61).

27. Berlinerblau rejects the notion of a distinct and inferior "popular religion." I agree. He suggests that "an elitist literati may *intentionally misrepresent* the religious beliefs of all other groups . . . [and] their views on the religion of other classes and groups will inevitably be pejorative and misleading" (Berlinerblau 1993, 13–14).

insignificant" (Fontaine 1988, 503).[28] She is then not a goddess. She is just a personification. She becomes thereby less than real. She is less important. In ancient times, they imply, nobody actually believed that she existed.

If it could be demonstrated that no Israelites took Hokmah seriously, she would no longer constitute a threat to monotheism. When Fontaine and others use the term "mere," they imply that a literary form of communication is inherently inferior, a container that holds less truth. It is the fancy of a single author used to convey a thought, because no one truly thinks of Hokmah as real. It (she) is an old idea from Israel's distant past, which a biblical author dredged up for literary effect.

In Proverbs 8, Hokmah is not an emanation of God, but rather Yahweh's daughter. The writing is mythological and not hypostatic. I contend that hypostatization, as expressed in the deuterocanon and later, does not weaken Hokmah's influence, but rather translates Hokmah into a new environment. These later eras require that the language of radical monotheism must be used, but the rigor of exclusivity no longer controls their imagination. Rich divine figures may be described as long as they are hypostatically linked to the one true God.

Hokmah the Goddess: Characteristically Israelite

In summary, by the Persian period, the vibrant figure of Hokmah troubled and threatened some, but they did not respond by excising her from the literature. Nor did they cut the guts out of her story, leaving her as an obscure reference. Rather, they provided a reinterpretation of her that allowed knowledge of her and her influence to continue. Moreover, contemporary interpreters did not want "official" Israel identified with a deity other than Yahweh, nor did they want late Israel identified with other gods. Therefore, they diminished her in two ways, by declaring her non-Israelite (early or foreign), or by relegating her to the status of "mere" literary device or hypostasis.

But why distance oneself from the obvious conclusion that the goddess is alive and well throughout the Israelite literature? Such a conclusion should not surprise us. Israelites could never agree on what Yahweh's relationship to other gods was. In this book, I seek to demonstrate that some

---

28. Ultimately, Lang takes this position. He says: "Should one place our poems, therefore, in the supposedly safe, orthodox religious climate of the late post-exilic period, in which anything polytheistic and pagan had long since ceased to be appealing to the Jewish mind? In a period, therefore, in which the poet could start to 'play' with ancient mythology because it had lost its *religious* power over the mind while keeping its *aesthetic* fascination?" (Lang 1986, 115).

in Israel regarded Yahweh as first in a pantheon of gods, some who regarded Yahweh as the only legitimate god for the Israelites, and some, the radical monotheists, who believed Yahweh to be the only real God in existence. But Hokmah inhabited a world in which loyalty to Yahweh did not preclude taking rich delight in a goddess of wisdom. Lang asserts: "It is evident that the notion of a 'goddess of the king,' which was part of a widespread royal ideology, was also familiar in Israel and played a part in shaping the image of wisdom in Proverbs 8. In fact, Wisdom must have been the name, or one of the names, of the Israelite kings' divine patroness" (1986, 61). Camp suggests that "the female imagery operated in such a way as to make this a viable religious symbol in an era without a king. Far from being a peculiar or foreign element, it provided key points of linkage to both ethos and world view, creating one form of symbolic substitute for the monarch" (Camp 1985, 282).

Rich biblical theological imagery becomes the material for contemporary theologizing. This same biblical imagery also provides a sense of broad limits and constraints on such activity. What then might we say about Hokmah? She is female. She brings into divinity notions of the personal, the relational, the mystical, and the erotic. She enlarges our notion of what constitutes femaleness in that she is not known for traditional female roles—she is not mother, does not bring fertility, and has no children. The life that Hokmah brings is intellectual life. She is forceful and authoritarian, challenging her students to follow her teaching.

Her realms are the mythology of creation, but also in the classroom, the city square, and the world of government (Lang 1986, 55). Hokmah's divinity is not divorced from the earth. She delights in Yahweh, but she also (and ultimately) delights in humanity, in the *běnê ʾādām*.

She is not a solemn god. Rather, she is playful and erotic. She teases and entices her charges. Her childhood is both homey (a little girl playing around her father while he works) and mythic (his "work" is the creation of the universe). Many have identified her as a spokesperson for any number of principles: right speech, the wisdom of God, the wisdom of the natural order, the tradition of school teaching, human wisdom. Hokmah links all these realms—the divine realm, the human realm, and the natural realm—and she is the linked tradition that contains all of them.

Therefore, when I examine the pedigree of Hokmah, both her antiquity and the space she is said to inhabit, she appears little different from the other divine beings in ancient Near Eastern stories. She resembles them in her relationship to the chief male god figure, in her instructional role, and in her relationship to her students. Additionally, the circumstances of her birth and her method of self-declaratory address draw parallels with other ancient Near Eastern goddesses (M. S. Smith 1987, 94, 115–17). There is no shortage of wise goddesses in ancient Near Eastern writing, which indicates that a thick tradition lay behind the depiction of Hokmah in Proverbs.

Proverbs 8 presents Hokmah as an Israelite goddess, the daughter of Yahweh. In spite of a movement in Israel toward greater and greater consolidation of divine power in the one god Yahweh, Hokmah retained her presence and influence in Israel and in Judaism and Christianity that followed. One sees her presence in Proverbs 1–10, and she reappears throughout the Jewish and Christian traditions. Therefore, we see further evidence that ancient Israel did not hold to a uniformly radically monotheistic position as is usually imagined. That is, radical monotheism must not be understood as *the* Israelite identity. Hokmah was recoverable by Christian and Jewish communities as a means by which they imagined divine attributes not usually included in portrayals/constructions of God the Father.[29]

Hokmah needs to be within our horizon, contributing to the idea of divinity. Murphy calls Hokmah "the feminine in God" (1998, 280). If Hokmah joins with Yahweh in hypostatic union, then it must affect the way we construct, think about, and experience God. Two persons I remember from my childhood might express this. The first is TV news anchor Walter Cronkite, grandfather-like, with that round, bland face, perfectly trimmed moustache, and graying hair, telling us every night, "And that's the way it is," in that authoritative voice of his. The other is Mae West, film and stage comedienne of the twenties and thirties. She was seductive, playful, experienced, and very erotic (her films were made before the movie censors clamped down). We can think of these two images, Walter Cronkite and Mae West, as different ways to construe God.

I think that Hokmah can bring a bit more of Mae West into the picture, and that would be a good thing.

---

29. Mark Smith observes, "Whether an indigenous development or a foreign import, these practices were allowed by the Judean dynasty at times to take place within the cult of its national god" (1987, 117).

Chapter 7

Lady Zion

The Beautiful Goddess

K ing Solomon built his temple on Mount Zion, a hilly protuberance
on the eastern side of the Old City of Jerusalem. It is likely that the
inhabitants of the land had long regarded it as a holy site. Traditions arose
that associated Zion with the major events in Israel's past. At Zion, people said, Yahweh turned back a plague because of the importuning of King
David (2 Sam. 24). Abraham offered his son on this mountain. Later traditions even identified Zion as the burial place of the first human.

Zion functions within the Psalter (and in other portions of Scripture)
as more than the geographical hill located in Jerusalem.[1] Mountains,
rivers, and temples represented their heavenly counterparts in the world
of the gods. For the Israelites, the land of Palestine, although small and
insignificant, was, in reality, the center of the universe. Eventually everyone would recognize that fact.

With this in mind, it is not surprising to note some rather extravagant
claims made for this moderate hill in central Palestine. Some of Israel's
poetic writings express and describe Zion as the highest mountain in
the world, from which the rivers of paradise flowed, the scene of the defeat
of chaos and of the pagan nations, and the object of an international

---

1. Pellett observes the difference between the appearance of the land and its significance: "A
geographer understands that landscape includes both the physical features and how these features appear to the observer. The vision may differ from the objective reality, yet the vision may
be more influential and have its own reality" (Pellett 1973, 272). Bibical scholars have begun
considering space as a theological category. The "Constructions of Ancient Space" seminar
and their publications provide the background for my discussion here. I recommend Berquist
2003 and Camp 2003. In addition, I recommend James W. Flanagan's online article listed in the
bibliography.

pilgrimage.[2] The people of Israel seemed untroubled by the incongruity of these ascriptions. The actual location of Zion fades into irrelevance as the poets wax eloquent concerning its (or her) majesty and glory. In Psalm 48:2 we read, "Mount Zion, in the far north," and in 133:3, "It is like the dew of Hermon, which falls on the mountains of Zion" (Pellett 1973, 274). The physical Mount Zion is not in the "far north," and nowhere near Mount Hermon. The word for "north," *ṣāpōn*, has definite mythological as well as geographical references. *Ṣāpōn* is also a place name, Baal Zaphon, now called Mount Cassius, north of Palestine. In the Canaanite tables at Ras Shamra, this mountain became the dwelling place of Baal (or El).

One might think that these grandiose ideas came from a small-minded people compensating for their inferiority. Zion, the spiritual center of Judean religion, is the center of the world in this poetry of the Psalms. The origin of a spiritual Zion is considerably more complex than that. The Israelites shared in common the idea of a divine and beautiful mountain-city with the other West Semitic cultures that surrounded them. While changing and adapting this mythology for their own use, the Judeans were deeply influenced by those traditions. The biblical Zion tradition managed a curious marriage between the religion of an ancient Jebusite (non-Israelite) shrine in Jerusalem and the religion of Israel. Many scholars believe that the account in 1 Chronicles 15 describes David cutting a deal with the Jebusite priesthood so that thereafter two guilds of priestly functionaries would direct activities in the temple (Roberts 1973, 335; cf. Dahood 1994, 290).[3]

When David brought the ark to Jerusalem, his newly conquered city, he organized a meeting between "the sons of Aaron and the Levites" on the one hand, and the priest Zadok. Presumably, Zadok represents the native, non-Israelite priesthood that oversaw the Jerusalem cult before David conquered the city, and the sons of Aaron and the Levites represent the priestly guild that had control of the cult outside of Jerusalem and was (in contrast to Zadok) of native Israelite stock. David joined together Canaanite and Israelite cult in the place he prepared for the ark.

David gives special jobs to the sons of Aaron, such as carrying the ark in processions. The Levites are given responsibility for music in the temple. The text does not say what those in the Zadok faction were given; perhaps they had oversight of the sacrifice in the sacred tent. At the end of

2. Roberts 1973, 329. See also Roberts 1976, 985.

3. It is assumed that Zadok is a Jebusite name, as in Melchi*zedek* in Gen. 14:18 (describing the priest of [Jeru]Salem) and King Adoni-*zedek* in Josh. 10:1, 3.

David's career, his court split in the choice of which of his sons would suc-
ceed him. The Zadok faction supported the claims of Solomon, the son
of Bathsheba, the favored wife. Abiathar (the leader of the "sons of
Aaron") supported Adonijah, the oldest surviving son. Because Solomon
became king, the Zadokites remained in the ascendancy for many years,
perhaps until the destruction of the temple in 587 BCE. This means that
a non-Israelite urban priesthood (the Zadokites) with a typical West
Semitic city-mythology significantly influenced the Yahweh religion that
established itself in Jerusalem.

In his great Psalms commentary, Kraus observes:

> Two different worlds met on Mount Zion: Israel's central sanctuary
> and the Canaanite cult of the holy city of Jerusalem. The Canaanite-
> Jebusite traditions were firmly rooted in this holy place. . . . These
> alien elements had to be taken up into the worship of Israel, trans-
> formed and incorporated into the service of Yahweh. (1988, 201)

Psalms 46 and 48 serve as good examples of the mythological use of the
Zion motifs.[4] In Psalm 46, in the midst of a violent scene where the waters
of chaos threaten to overwhelm the people of God, the psalmist writes,
"There is a river whose streams make glad the city of God, / the holy habi-
tation of the Most High [*elyôn*]" (v. 4). "City of God" here serves as a substitute for Zion, God's holy dwelling. A river streaming forth from a holy
city is a common ancient Near Eastern mythological motif. Here the
psalmist describes Zion as a lush city, the dwelling of Elyon. Streams proceed from its center, water the land, and bestow fertility.

In Psalm 48, the poet exclaims:

> Great is the LORD and greatly to be praised
>   in the city of our God.
> His holy mountain, beautiful in elevation,
>   is the joy of all the earth,
> Mount Zion, in the far north.
>
> (vv. 1–2)

The city of God is a mountain, standing tall among the mountains of
the earth, from which flows a life-giving stream. One might compare the

---

4. Kraus and others identify the Zion psalms as 46, 48, 76, 84, 87, 122, and perhaps 137. The
term "Zion songs" comes from Psalm 137 (Kraus 1988, 210).

religious importance of such an image to the role that Mount Olympus played for the ancient Greeks, who regarded their mountain as the highest of the mountains, the center of the earth (A. Robinson 1974, 121). When the psalmist referred to Zion located in distant *ṣāpōn* (in the far north), he transferred the significance of Baal Zaphon to the dwelling place of Yahweh in the temple in Jerusalem. Judeans thereby affirmed their belief that Yahweh was the supreme God and that his dwelling place was supreme over all the earth.

This mythological idea took on eschatological implications in Isaiah's prophecy. Isaiah likely walked up Mount Zion daily and knew it to be a modest hill. But in a time of crisis, he spoke of what it would become in the future:

> In days to come
>   the mountain of the LORD's house
> shall be established as the highest of the mountains,
>   and shall be raised above the hills;
> all the nations shall stream to it.
>
> (Isa. 2:2)

The Israelites regarded their mountain as the center of the earth, the highest of mountains, "the joy of all the earth," if not in a physical sense, then in a metaphorical sense that gave them a sense of place and purpose within their cosmos (Kraus 1966, 202). Joined with this image is the idea of streams of water flowing from this city of God. This too has parallels within the ancient Near Eastern world (Gibson 1977, 110; cf. Schmid 1955, 187). The idea of a river flowing from a garden city is closely tied to the Near Eastern concept of paradise. The waters were a source of life and fertility, and the paradisaical waters that flow from the city point to this place as the primary site where God meets with his people. Harrelson observes: "It seems fairly clear from a number of Old Testament passages (Ez. 28, Is. 14:12–14, Ps. 46, Is. 2:2–4 and Mic. 4:1–4) that a West Semitic version of the mountain city was known and used by Israel. According to this story, a city was built by the gods upon the highest mountain. From the city flowed the waters of life; there was located the tree of life" (1970, 247).[5]

---

5. Kelly 1968, 403. Kelly also observes, "Vertically, it is where the upper and lower worlds communicate, and as such participates in the great gift of both, to wit, the upper and lower waters which fertilize the earth and distribute food to it" (1968, 407). See also Harrelson 1969, 86.

This high, life-giving mountain was known in many cultures as "the navel of the earth," the world tree, the axis at the heart of the earth. It provided a mediating channel between the god(s) and the cosmos and gave the living water that brings forth the fertility of the world.[6] Often this mythical mountain stronghold became in the thinking of ancient peoples a god (Roberts 1973, 334). The Israelites personified Zion in this fashion.

These mythological themes in specific Zion psalms have a relationship to similar themes in other cognate cultures. In these other cultures, the people regarded these mountain cities as female gods. Maier observes regarding Zion as a female figure:

> [She] stems from a West-Semitic tradition depicting a city as female both grammatically and symbolically[,] . . . depicting the relationship of the city and its inhabitants as female roles: in relation to its ruler Jerusalem would be possessed like a woman; in relation to its inhabitants she would provide shelter and food like a mother for her children; and in relation to God, the title "daughter" would imply her need for protection. (2003, 9)

The most obvious connection between the mountain city and a feminine deity is the concept of fertility. Fertility comes from the river of life that flows from the city. In West Semitic thought, agricultural fertility was connected to the activities of female gods. The earth brings forth its fruit, and this parallels the process of pregnancy and birth. The earth was seen as the mother, as the source of all fecundity.[7] Fertility-bringing water comes from the Great Mother Goddess, who is a source for such water (Kraus 1966, 202).

This idea of water or the source of water as the Mother Goddess is further supported by ancient texts that W. F. Albright brought to the attention of the scholarly community early in the twentieth century. He states: "Here according to an ancient idea, there was a mighty river whence all

---

6. Kelly 1968, 403. Kelly also notes other passages of Scripture that point to this life-giving water coming to Israel from both the heavenly and underworld water systems. See Deut. 33:13; Gen. 49:25; Ps. 104:13; Ps. 133; Mal. 3:10; Zech. 14:16. Psalm 87:7 pronounces "All my springs are in you." This is important when one understands the world mountain as being the link between heaven and earth, between the heavenly and earthly waters (408).

7. Harrelson associates fertility with Zion when he notes: "Nations would flow up to Jerusalem, as once the waters of earth flowed from the city atop the highest mountain. Streaming back to the source of life and blessing, they would find their true life there" (Harrelson 1969, 141).

streams spring . . . [,] [the] river, creatress of everything, corresponding to the Sumerian goddess Engar . . . [,] mother who bore heaven and earth. This river [is] called . . . 'river of fertility'" (Albright 1919, 166–67). He goes on to suggest: "The source of the waters is also conceived of as the vagina of the earth mother who bears vegetation after nine months gestation" (168). Garden imagery in ancient literature has always stood for feminine sexuality. "A garden locked is my sister, my bride, / a garden locked, a fountain sealed" (Song 4:12). "My beloved [the male lover] has gone down to his garden . . . to gather lilies" (Song 6:2). Her lover gains sexual access by climbing over the wall and picking her fruit.

In the Psalter, praise to Zion is considered equivalent to praise for Yahweh, while in other psalms it is clear that the designation "Zion" refers to the people of Jerusalem or of Israel in general. Zion is spoken of as "beautiful in elevation" (Ps. 48:2). We might paraphrase this as "a majestically tall mountain." She is called "lovely," as the dwelling place of Yahweh in Psalm 84:1. Yet Zion is also challenged to praise God, and is spoken of as beloved of Yahweh. "Let Mount Zion be glad . . . because of your judgments" (Ps. 48:11). "The LORD loves the gates of Zion" (Ps. 87:2). There is also mention in Psalm 149:2 of *běnê-ṣiyyôn* ("Zion's children," perhaps meaning citizens of Jerusalem) and in Psalm 9:14 of *bat-ṣiyyôn* ("daughter of Zion," or more likely, "Daughter Zion," that is, Yahweh's daughter).[8]

Mowinckel and others suggest that praise to Zion indirectly praises Yahweh and recounts God's benefits given to the city. "It is because he is there and reveals himself and does his beneficial works of victory and deliverance that glorious things can be spoken of Zion" (Mowinckel 1962, 90). I believe that this does not exhaust the meaning of "Daughter Zion."

The psalmist calls Zion beautiful. God's mountain is "beautiful in elevation" (Ps. 48:2), "the perfection of beauty" (Ps. 50:2). The word for beauty, *yěpēh*, almost always refers to women, either figuratively or literally. In cases where it refers to men or objects, it seems to convey what we mean in English if we describe a man as "beautiful" rather than "handsome" or "good-looking."[9] Von Rad claims that the "beauty" of Zion is only a result of God's choice (1962, 46–47). This is certainly a factor, but

8. W. F. Stinespring argues articulately for the second phrase to be translated as "Maiden Zion" (1965, 133–41). In either case, Maiden Zion or daughter of Zion, the fundamental femininity of Zion is maintained.

9. The Bible uses this term fifty-six times. Thirty-two of those times it refers directly to women, ten times to men. The rest of the occurrences refer to objects or abstract ideas.

again I am not sure that it fully explains the ascription. Yahweh loves Zion, and she is beloved of her people, admired by both and seeming to share the qualities of both. Her beauty seems to have some independence from both Yahweh and the people of Israel.[10]

A brief survey of Jewish and Christian traditions supports the image of Zion/Jerusalem/the holy city/mountain as a feminine figure. In the rabbinical tradition, the stone in the holiest place in the temple holds back the *tĕhôm* (the primal waters of the deep), and the rabbis call these lower waters "the bride," while the upper waters are designated as the "bridegroom" (Patai 1976b, 55–59, 67). In the book of Revelation, John portrays Jerusalem as "a bride adorned for her husband" (Rev. 21:2).

There are three stages in the development of this Lady Zion theology. First, there is the Jebusite (pre-David Jerusalem) myth of Lady Zion, which is separate from the Israelite religion. Second, David incorporates Zion theology in support of his own claim to the throne. Jerusalem was David's city. Therefore, when the supporters of David's dynasty elevated the religious and symbolic importance of the city, it enhanced David's own position and hold on power, and that of his family. David's people identified Zion with "the city of David." Terrien claims that this Zion myth functioned to support the election of David to the monarchy: "Based originally on the Jebusite myth of the navel of the earth, the Zion theology became historicized into a theology of the election of David and Jerusalem" (Terrien 1970, 332). In the third stage in development of this idea, as the Israelite elite lost access to the physical Zion because of the exile, they tended to romanticize her beauty more and more. Pellett notes: "During the exile we can see how physical separation from Jerusalem increased rather than decreased devotion of the Jews for their holy city. . . . One way was to idealize the destroyed city and to move it into the realm of the mind and the heart where it would be invincible" (1973, 277).[11]

Lady Zion served as a mediatrix between Yahweh and his people. She "humanized" Yahweh's qualities and served as an object of devotion and love for the people. She was somehow less transcendent and more available than the ineffable God. During the exile, she served as the link to the home for which the exiles longed and the God that they worshiped.

10. Stolz describes her as "the embodiment of beauty and the center of the world" (1976, 543).

11. Pellett states, "Before 586 BC, the city was *officially* holy, but afterwards it was to achieve an *authentic* holiness, to become in the imagination of its exiles the seat of all virtues and a mirror of heaven" (1973, 277).

Even in their bitterness, they remembered her and the songs she inspired in them.

Zion is a minor Israelite deity, female, beautiful, a source of fertility. The citizens of the city are her children. The Israelites connected her with images of mountain, river, and city combined.

A displaced temple singer penned these words about his beloved lady:

> By the rivers of Babylon—
>   there we sat down and there we wept
>   when we remembered Zion.
> . . . .
> If I forget you, O Jerusalem,
>   let my right hand wither!
> Let my tongue cling to the roof of my mouth,
>   if I do not remember you,
>   if I do not set Jerusalem
>   above my highest joy.

Chapter 8

Asherah and Archaeology

D oes Yahweh have a wife? The writer of Genesis 1 vehemently denies it. He declares that God is both male and female and thus neither needs nor desires sexual companionship (Gen. 1:27). But did all Israel agree? A surface reading of the Hebrew Bible would suggest that those who believed that gods had wives were the foreigners and those who had completely fallen away from the Israelite faith. But that is not correct.

In previous chapters I have limited my inquiry to actual texts within the Hebrew Bible. In this chapter I cast my net wider and examine some of the evidence from archaeology, the physical and written remains of ancient Israel and its neighbors. Whereas the Bible has passed through many hands before reaching us, archaeology provides data that no subsequent editor had opportunity to change. But in this case, both archaeology and ancient biblical texts agree that some Israelites believed that Yahweh had a wife, usually named Asherah. In this chapter, I will examine the biblical evidence for Asherah and then demonstrate how we might modify our understanding by what archaeologists have found in various sites in Palestine and surrounding regions.

The Biblical Evidence

There is no one Asherah in the Hebrew Bible. Some references to Asherah refer to a divine female figure worshiped by Israelite royalty and foreigners living in Israel.[1] In 1 Kings 18:19 we read of the "four hundred

---

1. See 1 Kgs. 15:13; 2 Kgs. 21:7; 23:4. See also Judg. 3:7, in which the plural form *Asheroth* is used (J. Day 1992, 485).

fifty prophets of Baal and the four hundred prophets of Asherah, who eat at Jezebel's table." Jezebel was a Phoenician princess who married Ahab, before he became the king of Israel. Subsequently, she became Israel's queen. The Hebrew narratives depict her as a strong advocate of the worship of Baal. The author identifies Baal as the god of her people. Jezebel actively persecuted the followers of Yahweh, particularly Yahweh's prophets. Elijah, one of Yahweh's prophets, challenged the prophets of Baal to a duel; whoever's god would send down fire from the sky would win the contest. The prophets of Asherah do nothing in the story. When Elijah defeats Baal's prophets in the contest, he orders their mass execution, but he does not have the Asherah prophets murdered. There are various explanations for this inactivity. Some suggest that the mention of Asherah's prophets is an addition to the story and that some editor (one who had an Asherah axe to grind) inelegantly added this line while not changing the story to fit.[2]

I want to suggest another explanation, one that does not presume an editorial misstep. In such a divine contest, Asherah would have constituted no threat to the worship of Yahweh. In effect, two male gods were competing for supremacy, and perhaps Asherah was the prize of the successful male god. The text remains ambiguous on this point. Two males competing over a woman does not make a pretty scene. The combatants (Yahweh and Baal) seem like oversexed adolescents, and it diminishes the woman. But alas, the reputed old adage "as on earth, so in heaven," works the opposite way as well. The behavior of the gods reflects the unjust patriarchy on earth.

We find a number of other places where the term "Asherah" in the Bible refers to the female goddess. The accounts of the Israelite kings sometimes describe certain religious objects that represented Asherah the goddess, or were erected on her behalf. In describing King Asa of Judah, the author recounted how he "also removed his mother Maacah from being queen mother, because she had made an abominable image for Asherah" (1 Kgs. 15:13). If Maacah made an image *for* Asherah, Asherah would not be the image but the goddess behind the image. We therefore might conclude that the goddess Asherah is present in the Bible, though indistinct and subservient. But that is not the only way the Bible uses this word.

---

2. "The facts that the prophets of Asherah play no part in the subsequent story in 1 Kings 18 suggest that the reference to them may be a gloss. However, the parallelism with the prophets of Baal makes it natural to suppose that whoever added the gloss about the prophets of Asherah understood Asherah to be the name of a deity" (J. Day 1992, 485).

More commonly in the Bible, "Asherah" refers to a cult object, probably a wooden pole, that symbolizes a tree.[3] For example, in the account of King Ahab of Israel, it says, "He erected an altar for Baal in the house of Baal, which he built in Samaria. Ahab also made a sacred pole [*Asherah*]" (1 Kgs. 16:32–33). Periodically, southern kings would object to these Asherah cult objects, would have them destroyed, and would punish their defenders: "[Hezekiah] did what was right in the sight of the LORD just as his ancestor David had done. He removed the high places, broke down the pillars, and cut down the sacred pole [*Asherah*]" (2 Kgs. 18:3–4).

Some assert that these poles were of foreign origin. For reasons I will discuss below, such an accusation is misplaced. These were native Israelite activities and objects. I contend that when some of the writers of the Bible accuse Asherah poles of coming by way of foreign influence, they are trying to demonize an opponent's position. The ones in Israel who opposed the poles appear to be those of the Yahweh-alone party. For most of the time, however, these objects were tolerated and even cherished in Israelite sacred spaces, particularly by the royal families.

However, almost all biblical material has been written through the lens of those who actively opposed the worship of Asherah or her cult objects. Therefore, likely much has been cut out of the account, particularly those texts sympathetic to or tolerant of Asherah. What remains is negative, and therefore we must look elsewhere to gain a complete picture of the nature of Asherah piety in ancient Israel.

The Deuteronomic History (Joshua–2 Kings) for the most part regards Asherah as foreign pollution that the leaders of Israel must eradicate if they are to worship Yahweh in purity. Fortunately for us, we have more information than what exists in the heavily edited and ideologically laden Bible. That Bible was being formed at the time when a particular religious viewpoint was being imposed upon the whole. "One ought not . . . to confuse the minority opinion expressed in the religious literature preserved in the Old Testament with the historic religion of Israel in the pre-exilic period" (M. Weippert, quoted in Keel and Uehlinger 1992, 3).[4]

---

3. The following words are used for the production of the Asherah pole:

Make: 1 Kgs. 14:15; 16:33; 2 Kgs. 17:10, 16; 21:3; Isa. 17:8; 2 Chr. 33:3
Build: 1 Kgs. 14:23
Erect: 2 Kgs. 17:19; 2 Chr. 33:19
See Olyan 1988, 1–2, and J. Day 1992, 486.

4. "According to M. Weippert, biblical texts, such as Psalms 82, 89 and Deut 32:8f, indicate 'that even the "official" theology of the Jerusalem Temple itself was neither a monolatry nor a monotheism even in the late pre-exilic era, but was simply polytheistic'" (Weippert, quoted in Keel and Uehlinger 1992, 2–3).

The Archaeological Evidence

Asherah is the name of a goddess commonly known throughout the region of the ancient Near East during the period of the writing of the Hebrew Bible.[5] The figure of Asherah appears widely throughout the mythological stories of the ancient Near East. For example, the Ras Shamra mythological stories mention Asherah as the consort (wife) of ʾēl or Baal.[6] Archaeologists discovered this treasure trove of Canaanite writings on the Syrian coast. These clay tablets date from a few hundred years before the rise of the Israelite monarchy (the fourteenth through the thirteenth centuries). In the Ras Shamra tablets, ʾēl is the father god who rules over the other gods. Most of the occurrences of the word ʾēl in the Bible are translated as "God," virtually synonymous with the use of the term "Yahweh," but in the Ras Shamra texts, ʾēl is the chief god and Asherah is his consort. It is not a great leap, therefore, to wonder if there is any evidence that as Yahweh "subsumed" ʾēl, taking over his power and functions (see chapter 5), he also took as his own ʾēl's consort Asherah. Is there any archaeological evidence that Asherah is a consort of Yahweh? The answer is yes. As Keel and Uehlinger observe:

> In the four and a half centuries during which there were one or two Israelite monarchies (ca. 1020–586 B.C.), there was a dominant polytheistic religion that was indistinguishable from that of neighboring peoples. Insofar as there were differences . . . *these beliefs stayed within the framework of Near Eastern polytheism* [emphasis added] and each should be interpreted as a local variant of the same basic pattern. (Keel and Uehlinger 1992)[7]

Kuntillet ʿAjrûd, Khirbet el-Qom, and Elephantine

Central to any examination of ancient Israel's relationship to the goddess Asherah, one must consider the discoveries at two sites in southern Pales-

---

5. One finds similar accounts of Asherah as chief female deity in Akkadian accounts as well as Egyptian and Hittite sources (see J. Day 1992, 483–87).

6. For a general discussion of Ras Shamra, see Mayes 1997, 63; Albright 1957, 231; Frymer-Kensky 1992, 158.

7. They go on to say: "The Israelites . . . venerated their own protector god who was there to provide for health and family. But they venerated Yahweh as well, the regional and national god, whose special domain dealt with war and peace issues. Finally, they worshiped gods who performed specific functions, those that were responsible for various special needs, weather, rain, woman's fertility, etc." (Keel and Uehlinger 2; see also Lang 1983, 20.)

tine dating from the tenth century BCE, which would roughly correspond to the period just before the Israelite monarchy. At Kuntillet ʿAjrûd in the Sinai,[8] archaeologists have discovered a small structure that some have thought a temple, but it was more likely a way station on the trade route from Palestine to Egypt. Archaeologists have also discovered *pithoi* (large ceramic pots) in Kuntillet ʿAjrûd. One pithos has inscribed on it some illustrations and writing. Scholars have not agreed on the meaning of these words and pictures. (The pictures are ambiguous and might not be related to the writing at all. They will figure no further in this discussion.) Written on the pottery is this simple prayer or invocation of protection: "I have blessed you by Yahweh of Samaria and his Asherah."[9] The meaning of the key phrase, "Yahweh and his Asherah," remains a much disputed point among interpreters. Susan Ackerman correctly concludes: "Choosing between 'his Asherah' and 'his asherah' cannot at this point, it seems, be decided. But for our purposes, it does not really matter. In the ancient Near East the idol was the god" (Ackerman 1989, 65).[10]

Olyan concurs:

> The biblical evidence . . . suggests that the asherah was a cult symbol representing the goddess Asherah which was an acceptable and legitimate part of Yahweh's cult. . . . This association of the asherah and the cult of Yahweh suggests in turn that Asherah was the consort of Yahweh in circles both in the north and the south. (Olyan 1988, 33)

Earlier in this chapter I pointed out that in the Bible the term "Asherah" means two different things: either a goddess or a wooden pole,

8. Kuntillet ʿAjrûd is located in the eastern Sinai fifty kilometers south of Kadesh Barnea, and Khirbet el-Qom, ten kilometers east-southeast of Lachish (Ackerman 1989, 62).

9. This translation is from J. Day 1992, 484. This is how Ackerman translates the important phrases: "At Kuntillet ʿAjrud, the excavator, Z. Meshel, has discovered a ninth- or eighth-century sanctuary (located on a pilgrimage route?), which has yielded three sensational inscriptions (on pithoi)

1) 'I bless you by Yahweh of Samaria and by his Asherah/asherah.'

2) 'Yahweh of the south and his Asherah/asherah.'

3) 'I bless you by Yahweh and his Asherah/asherah may he bless you and keep you and be with my lord.'" (Ackerman 1989, 62–63)

10. She goes on to say: "[It] . . . could refer to Asherah's cult object, the stylized tree, or even to some hypostasized aspect of the female side of Yahweh. But what was the stylized tree or the hypostasis of the female side of Yahweh to the average worshiper in ancient Israel? Nothing other than Asherah, the goddess. To associate Yahweh with Asherah's cult object or with some hypostasized female aspect of Yahweh is to associate Yahweh with Asherah" (Ackerman 1989, 65-66).

either a thing or a divine being. The form of the phrase "his Asherah" would be unusual in Hebrew if it were a proper name. This has been used as an argument that "Asherah" in these inscriptions refers to the cult object and not to the goddess. "Yahweh and his Asherah" would then mean "Yahweh and the cult object that has been dedicated to him." The implication is that the word "Asherah" has lost all connection with the goddess, and now constitutes no challenge to monotheism. But as I have shown, even when the text refers to "Asherah" as a wooden pole, it still refers back to the goddess whom the pole represents.[11]

Complicating things further, if "Asherah" is a thing, it seems odd that some long-forgotten Israelite invoked the protection of a cult object and did not rather invoke the protection of the god alone.[12] In any case, the Israelite God Yahweh became associated with "Asherah," a term that everywhere else in the ancient Near East referred to a supreme female goddess.

Khirbet el-Qom, a site in the Judean hill country to the north of Kuntillet ʿAjrûd, contains similar invocations, this time written on the wall of a tomb. In this inscription, the writer speaks for Uriyahu, asking Yahweh to act on his behalf "for the sake of his Asherah."[13] This phrase suggests that Yahweh is more powerful than Asherah and that Yahweh and Asherah are in relationship. Zevit offers useful insights into this text when he observes: "The nature of the incantation [in the el-Qom site] suggests that the goddess herself did not or could not save; it was not within her bailiwick. This may have been because she was not a healing goddess. Still, she stood in such a relationship to YHWH, a healer, that an appeal invoking her name could save [Uriyahu]" (Zevit 2001, 369). Zevit presumes that Uriyahu must have been an Asherah devotee and that is why it would be for Asherah's sake (to her benefit) that Uriyahu must be saved (369). No other explanation is equally plausible. Therefore, we might conclude that for at least some Israelites, Yahweh had a consort named Asherah. Zevit observes, "The mythology underlying all of this can only have indicated

11. Some observe that "his Asherah" must refer to a thing, because Hebrew does not put a possessive pronoun as a suffix on the end of proper nouns. The evidence from the Hebrew is sketchy, and other ancient Semitic languages and some dialects of modern Arabic do put possessive pronouns on the end of proper nouns (Schmidt 1995, 97).

12. Compare this with the Israelite practice of swearing by the temple or the altar in Jerusalem (Matt. 5:34–37; 23:16–22).

13. The quote from Khirbet el-Qom says, "Uriyahu the rich wrote it. / Blessed be Uriyahu by Yahweh. / For from his enemies by his Asherah he has saved him / by Oniyahu / and by his Asherah" (J. Day 1992, 484–85).

that both deities [Yahweh and Asherah] were powerful, known to each other, and operated in the same sphere" (309). Miller has aptly noted that this evidence is "hardly what one would expect in a Yahwistic context" (Miller 2000, n. 3). In Kuntillet ʿAjrûd, the name Yahweh is connected with Samaria and Teman, both located within the territory of Israel (J. Day 1992, 485).

An additional reference was found in the remains of a Jewish community a few hundred miles to the south and a few hundred years later in time. Elephantine is an island in the Nile River, located just north of the first cataract, upstream (south) from the Nile Delta.[14] In the fifth century, a small Jewish colony lived on the island. Archaeologists have discovered a quantity of papyri at this site. These writings indicate that the Elephantine Jewish community remained unaffected by the monotheistic reforms that had taken place in Palestine. Although Judean kings based in Jerusalem had suppressed religious shrines throughout the country, this group of Judeans had built their own temple in which they worshiped Yahweh. They worshiped other gods as well, although Yahweh was stronger and more important. Might we not have in Elephantine an unedited picture of large-scale Israelite belief in a goddess as Yahweh's consort, when not seen through the filter of the Yahweh-alone party? We see in all these examples—Elephantine, Kuntillet ʿAjrûd, and Khirbet el-Qom—a society in which loyalty to Yahweh does not require that we empty the pantheon of all except Yahweh.

Female Cult Figures

Thousands of small statues have been found in Israelite households in all periods of their history. These figures usually have prominent breasts. Their arms are either straight out or positioned to display or offer their breasts, which was probably a maternal and not a sexual gesture. No ancient writing links these figures with Asherah, but there are good reasons to associate them with religious activity in connection with her worship. They are found in virtually every period of ancient Israelite and Judean history, although their popularity fell off considerably at certain moments. They appeared to function in family rather than temple settings. Zevit called them "prayers in clay," and Albright speculated that they were "nurturing goddesses" (Dever 1997, 52). Some have suggested

14. For a fuller discussion of Elephantine, see Keel and Uehlinger 1992, 386, and Hayes and Miller 1990, 486–87.

that the later statues did not represent goddesses but rather were non-divinized cult objects (51–53). Frymer-Kensky has observed: "They are a visual metaphor, which show in seeable and touchable form that which is most desired. In other words, they are a kind of tangible prayer for fertility and nourishment" (1992, 159). This is the same claim made for the asherah poles in the Bible, namely, that they are things unrelated to the goddess. That they are religious figures, nearly everyone agrees. Frymer-Kensky insists that they do not represent female deities but rather are things used in the worship of Yahweh with no separate meaning. She goes on to say:

> There is no evidence at all to suppose that the people imagined the figurines to represent God's consort. They have no pubic triangle, nothing to suggest erotic attachment, and they appear alone, not as part of a male-female couple[,] . . . not fully articulated or personified, not "worshiped" as some sort of a goddess that could rival YHWH. (160)

For a contrary perspective, consider a tenth-century cult stand found in Taanach, a town in northern Israel (J. Day 1992, 486). The second and fourth layers of this stand (which might have held incense or a small vegetable offering) parallel each other visually. The one depicts a tree flanked by two ibexes; the other contains a nude female figure with a lion on either side. Dever raises the question and then answers it: "Who is this enigmatic figure? She can be no other than Asherah, the Canaanite mother goddess. Asherah is known throughout the Levant in this period as the 'Lion Lady,' and she is often depicted nude, riding on the back of a lion" (1997, 35). The two different images go together. They depict the same figure in two different representations. Asherah is the tree and the female figure.

Let us review the evidence before us: (a) Asherah is identified as a pole, or is represented by a pole in the Bible; (b) there are widespread appearances of Asherah as a major goddess figure throughout the ancient Near East; (c) in many sites in ancient Israel, there are female figurines, in which frequently the lower body is represented by a pole; (d) there are two parallel figures on a cult stand: one a tree, another a nude, standing goddess figure, with common Asherah iconography; and (e) the inscriptions occur on a number of occasions linking Yahweh to ("his") Asherah. We might therefore make the following inference: tree = goddess = Asherah. Dever draws this conclusion:

Considering that we have only a handful of ancient Hebrew inscriptions from tombs or cultic contexts, the fact that two of them mention "A/asherah" in the context of a blessing is striking. It would appear that in nonbiblical texts such an expression was common, *an acceptable expression of Israelite Yahwism* [emphasis added] throughout much of the monarchy. (Dever 1997, 45)

Some Contrary Evidence

On the basis of the archaeological evidence, I suggest that Asherah held the important position of consort to Yahweh. We must now consider some of the objections to this position. There are two main ones. The first concerns the distribution of the figurines, and the second introduces new information from the ancient written material having to do with lists of names that have been discovered. Aside from the change in the style of the figurines,[15] one finds fewer of these figures coming from the period that roughly corresponds to King Josiah's religious reform. This parallels the biblical narrative: "The king commanded the high priest Hilkiah . . . to bring out of the temple of the LORD all the vessels made for Baal, *for Asherah* [emphasis added], and for all the host of heaven" (2 Kgs. 23:4). It appears that a widespread purging of Asherah objects took place, which would have included the figurines.

This king centralized worship in the temple in Jerusalem and eliminated many of the common cultic items that had previously been accepted as normal in the practice of worship. Along with these items, he destroyed the asherah poles (2 Kgs. 23:4–8). He initiated draconian measures that sought to eliminate the family/tribal religion that had existed for centuries outside of Jerusalem. Many fewer female figures are found in the ruins of Israelite houses from the time of Josiah (early seventh century BCE). Does that mean that Josiah wiped out Asherah worship? Ackerman insists that Josiah's reform was "limited in scope, temporary in effect, and clearly failed in its goal of impressing a monolithic description of Yahwism on all of Yahweh's devotees" (Ackerman 1989, 213). As proof, shortly afterward, these figures became popular again. Ackerman observes that the supporters of Josiah's reform "were not the only Yahwists of the sixth century" (214).

---

15. Whether a particular figurine has a lower body or a pole I conclude insignificant for whether or not it is a divine representation.

Some argue that the decline in distribution of the figurines indicates the "success" of monotheism. However, they are making a number of dubious assumptions. Taking at face value the idea that what has been found represents an accurate sampling of what actually existed in the ancient world, they assume that a drop in the number of figurines represents an actual loss in the popularity of Asherah piety.[16] That is a reasonable assumption, but other plausible ones also exist. A widespread government effort to suppress a religious practice could have resulted in a reduction of figurines without a significant change in local family piety.

For instance, the former Soviet Union worked for seventy-five years to stamp out Orthodox piety, represented by icons and images. An archaeologist excavating from that period (if such a thing were possible) would likely find a significant reduction in images. Would that find have indicated a significant reduction in piety? Perhaps, but following the fall of the Soviet Union, Orthodox piety returned with a vengeance, as if that seventy-five-year period of religious repression had never taken place.

The names that people in the region gave their children offer another bit of evidence that the people in Israel did not worship Asherah.[17] Names are found in personal letters, official documents and inscriptions, and official seals. How did parents in the ancient world choose names for their infants? Many assume that names represented the deepest beliefs of a people. Theophoric names (names that carry a name for god) are then thought to represent a people's most significant religious sensibilities.[18] In the ancient Near East, theophoric names were common.

---

16. Olyan disagrees: "In general, there is no direct correlation between the importance of the deities of the official cult (myths, pantheon lists and royal inscriptions) and the gods of popular piety, as reflected in person names and dedications" (1988, 35).

17. Miller notes that both in biblical and epigraphic names, names containing some form of "Yahweh" increased (Miller 1987, 243). "Up to the present time, not a single inscription from 7th or 6th century Judah has been found on which a goddess is mentioned by name" (Keel and Uehlinger 338). "These documents [on silver amulets] provide us with evidence for the existence of early exponents of a decidedly non-mythological movement that recognized neither Asherah nor another goddess, wanting instead to orient itself toward Yahweh and his temple alone" (Keel and Uehlinger 372).

18. "The predominance of names in the biblical texts that use 'Yahweh' or 'El' as their theophoric element virtually to the exclusion of other deities except possibly Baal should be seen to be the result of the same process of 'monotheisizing' inherited tradition" (Edelman 1995, 18). Keel writes:

Note Tigay's fundamental observations: "1) Names express the views of those who choose them, normally parents, and not necessarily of those who bear the names. 2) In Northwest

Throughout Israel's history, names carrying the theophoric elements *Yah*, *Yahu* (that is, Yahweh) or *El* (usually translated "God") were the most common from the eighth through the sixth centuries BCE. What does this mean? How do we interpret this data? It could mean (Tigay suggests, while many others proclaim) that during this period Israel was overwhelmingly, exclusively Yahwistic.[19] That is, by naming their children with these names, they showed their allegiance to the Yahweh-alone ideology. Keel therefore concludes that "personal piety in Israel (and Judah) was shaped by Yahwistic thinking and had aligned itself in a significant way with the 'official religion' of the Israelite state" (Keel and Uehlinger 1992, 206).

Tigay assumed that the theophoric names provide a window on ancient belief. He collected hundreds of objects with written names on them. He expected to find widespread use of theophoric prefixes and suffixes that contained the names of other gods. To his surprise, he found almost exclusively the use of *Yah* and *Yahu*.[20] But Tigay urges caution. He admits the *possibility* that this might mean that the Israelites worshiped no other gods, but he offers other explanations as well:

Semitic personal names, even members of polytheistic groups rarely invoke more than one deity in a single name. 3) The beliefs and attitudes expressed in Northwest Semitic personal names are simple and elemental. They express thanks for the god's beneficence, hope for his blessing and protection, submission to his authority, and the like. They are not theoretical, theological statements. After making the bold claim that Israelite names reflect a monotheistic mindset, Tigay undermines his whole thesis in an honest but ultimately self-defeating concession. Even if Israelite names throughout the biblical period were overwhelmingly Yahwistic, a point I do not concede, it might not (or would likely not) reflect a monotheistic belief. See also Keel and Uehlinger 204 n. 23.

19. McCarter argues from the absence of theophoric names, "that Israel in the Iron Age lost interest in the other gods. Moreover, the oldest literature preserved in the Bible, together with the scant corpus of texts that archaeologists have recovered from the Syro-Palestinian nation-states of the Iron Age, suggest that the divine was perceived as an essential singularity, with significant historical events being attributed to the will of the national god and no other" (1997, 73–74). Mayes sees the evidence as conclusive. He asserts that the evidence "suggests that Israel was an overwhelmingly Yahwistic society, to an extent that it would be justified to use the term 'monolatrous' of the religious practice of that society" (Mayes 1997, 52).

20. This is the account in Tigay's own words: "I expected to find on the Hebrew seals numerous examples of pagan personal names which were not found in the Bible because of the kind of scribal revisions which had turned Eshbaal into Ishbosheth and Beel(=Baal)iada into Eliada. But the index showed so few examples of such names that I was forced to wonder whether they had been as common as I had assumed and—since personal names are reflex of religious loyalties—whether polytheism was as prevalent among the Israelites as scholars believed" (1986, ix).

Even if the names of a particular society should reflect the predominance of a single deity to the total exclusion of all others, this would tell us only that members did not expect from other gods the kinds of action that are mentioned in personal names, and perhaps that they did not worship other gods. The absence of other gods from the onomasticon [name lists] would not by itself tell us whether the society denied the existence or divinity of those gods. (Tigay 1986, 6–7)

In a similar vein Keel observes, "The absence of the name of a goddess or of goddesses among the personal names that were used during Iron Age II cannot, in and of itself, convince someone that female deities played no important role in Israel during the eighth century" (Keel and Uehlinger 1992, 206). For instance, the naming might represent an effort on the part of the elite (or those who want to be) to emulate and support the efforts of the royal house to suppress traditional, locally based religion. It is likely that only the names of the rich and powerful were preserved in the tablets that have endured the millennia.[21]

Morton Smith draws the following conclusions:

> This is what we should expect of the Old Testament, given its character as a cult collection. It is concerned to heroize the patrons, priests, and prophets of the cult and to magnify the cult deity [Yahweh]. Of course the collectors did not include material in praise of competing deities and their patrons and personnel. (M. Smith 1971, 19)[22]

Smith creates the picture (accurately, in my opinion) of an Israel, through *all* of its history, that is extremely heterodox—that is, with many different positions on the major theological issues. Issues such as the following were vigorously debated in ancient Israel: How do we identify the national god? Is it alright to have family gods? What are the acceptable images by which

21. See Hess 2004 for a contrary view. Hess sees the crude nature of the handwriting as in some cases indicating a lower-class (and thus not elite) origin to some of the name lists.

22. He goes on: " For that material—psalms celebrating the tender mercies of Asherah, stories of the miracles worked by the prophets of Baal or of the zeal of the priests of Anath, histories of the poetry and devotion of Manasseh and Jezebel and of the reformations they effected in the national religion—for all this we can argue only from analogy. Only from analogy, too, can we guess at the polemics produced by the opposition—the denunciations of Jehu's murders (by the prophets of Baal) and of Josiah's sacrileges (by the priests of the . . . shrines)" (M. Smith 1971, 19).

we might approach the divine? Who are the authentic priests and prophets who bring the divine to us? What are the authentic places? Smith insists that with the Bible we have only one version, one side of the story ("given its character as a cult collection"). He rightly observes that there might likely be other versions, other sides.

He further observes that we must rethink the role of the "official" Israelite position, which I have characterized in this book as "radical monotheism," the belief that only one god exists and all other gods are delusional or demonic (or perhaps mere manifestations of the one true God). "Radical monotheism" characterizes only a small sliver of Israelite/Judean religious beliefs. The reason why radical monotheism dominates our readings of the Hebrew Bible (and subsequently has shaped rabbinic Judaism, Christianity, and Islam) is because a band of radical monotheists returned from Babylonian captivity and had the ear and the support of the Persian emperor (whose forces occupied Palestine).[23] They were able to edit the final version of the Hebrew Bible. Although they could not eliminate all the popular stories, laws, or poetry, they managed to get most of their own material in and to provide short (and not-so-short) editing remarks that shape and steer the way the subsequent stories are read.

Smith's greatest contribution to this inquiry was his introduction of the concept of the Yahweh-alone party. As he describes it, this was not just one group that operated monolithically, but a number of different groups working from different sets of interests. They combined to impose the conviction that Israel was to worship Yahweh alone. Some elements in this group had existed for a long time (such as Elijah's anti-Baal platform), while others came about as a direct result of the Persian occupation (the Judean priests who compiled lists and organizations of laws).[24] But they

---

23. Smith provides the following survey of the party's collusion with Persian authorities:

The leaders of the Yahweh-alone party seem to have been mostly carried off to Babylonia. There the party secured a strong and wealthy following among the exiles. At the time of the Persian conquest, it supported the Persians and thereafter succeeded in placing some of its members in high positions in the Persian court. With Persian support it eventually gained control of the rebuilt Jerusalem temple and then won over the populace, first of Jerusalem, later of Judea. This made it the largest and politically the most important group within the cult of Yahweh. Its preeminence was enhanced by the success of the literature which it produced or edited (most of the books now in the Old Testament) and by the traditional prestige of Jerusalem. (M. Smith 1971, 82–83)

24. I am indebted to Jon Berquist, particularly his *Judaism in Persia's Shadow*, for this insight into the role of the Persian occupiers in the development and codification of the Hebrew Bible.

all came together to produce the Hebrew Bible as we encounter it today (Smith 1971, 29).

Scholars have long debated what exact moment saw the end of polytheism as a viable religious system in the Israelite community. The more conservative would tend to place that point as early as possible, the times of Abraham and Moses being the chief candidates. What I am suggesting, and others seem to be hinting at, is that there was *never* a point at which polytheism ceased to be an option for an Israelite/Jew (at least up until the third century BCE, which is as far as my inquiry takes me).

Were there no changes in Israelite belief over these centuries? The Israelites and Jews had to respond to the domination of the Yahweh-alone party, the radical monotheists in the Second Temple, the ones who cooperated with the Persian occupiers. Most if not all of these changes, however, were *cosmetic* or *semantic* changes, while among the majority of the population the old belief system remained substantially the same. The word *ʾelōhîm*, as an example, had been previously used both as a name for a singular god (translated "god") and as a plural collection of divine beings (translated "gods"). In a concession to the Yahweh-alone movement, *ʾelōhîm* could now only be used to refer to Yahweh. The inhabitants of Persian-occupied Judah then and afterward in the various Jewish communities accommodated to monotheism without truly accepting its most radical premise—that all gods other than Yahweh were delusional (the position of Second Isaiah; see chapter 6).

Mark Smith suggests that most of the other gods in Israel either were assimilated into Yahweh and became part of his being, or else they became something considerably less than divine—angels, for instance (see M. S. Smith 1987; 2001). I suggest rather that divine beings other than Yahweh continued to be served and worshiped by mainstream Israelites or Jews, although they conceded certain things to the dominant ideology. As Ackerman observes:

> These worshipers [of Asherah] are never reported as rejecting Yahweh. They simply believed that it was legitimate in Yahwism to supplement the worship of Yahweh with the worship of other gods. Clearly this belief guided those who participated in the cult of Asherah, for they worshipped this goddess alongside Yahweh as his hypostatized female aspect or even consort. The definition of what constitutes proper Yahwism in popular religion, in short, encompasses far more than the definition of Yahwism proposed by the biblical writers would allow. (Ackerman 1989, 215)

The world presents itself to us in such a way that suggests both unified and diverse interpretations, that is, seeing behind the universe a single ruling principle versus seeing the universe as a struggle between many principles. Therefore, at a time when the dominant religious ideology of a society saw the universe as held together by a single unified principle (Yahweh alone), there naturally cropped up a strong impulse toward universe-as-struggle. One can understand this as an innate impulse to balance what had been misweighted, or else (as I mentioned in the introduction) one might see it as Freud's "return of the repressed," whereby that which has been actively banished from conscious reflection comes back with a vengeance by other means. Angels, demons, personified nature, personified wisdom, and, in this instance, Asherah are the other means.

Conclusion

This book represents a subversive reading. It challenges twenty-five centuries of tradition that has read the entire Bible with a monotheistic lens. Monotheism only works because it allows for modifications and qualifications. The Jewish, Christian, and Muslim gods have always made their way through conflict and struggle. Monotheism, however, must not be construed as the final destination of theology, the end of history. Rather, the contrary view to monotheism, polytheism, persists in pulling the church (and others) back from the abyss of monism, a horribly frigid place where nothing moves. Monism construes a world where everything gets sucked into a single vortex point. God in such a universe becomes so abstract and distant that various gods and godlike beings emerge to compensate.

How might I justify such a radical departure from conventional interpretations? I offer the following observations:

1. The actual texts of the Bible should offer feedback to the traditions that emerged from it. The Bible should act on some occasions as a corrective to traditionally held beliefs.
2. An analysis of these texts provides a backdrop and explanation for the complexities of monotheism that have been present throughout the history of this idea.
3. Some have suggested a direct relationship between radical monotheism and intolerant, oppressive attitudes toward other religious faiths. Regina Schwartz describes a religion of scarcity where there is not enough god to go around (1997, 33, 89–90, 114–17). Religions must compete for worship and worshipers, and ruthlessly suppress other faiths.

91

Perhaps a more open and complex view of divinity would promote a better understanding between religious faiths, particularly now, when we seem to be in each other's faces so often.

In order to be a Christian, one must be able to join in the historic affirmation that there is only one God. However, a Christian (at least) may believe that in many ways, this monotheism is complex. It is complicated by the belief in the Trinity. It is complicated by the belief in angels. It is complicated by the manifestation of the divine in the forces of nature. For Roman Catholics, it is complicated by devotion to Mary and the saints. The church's willingness to accept these complications, however, is what enables me to continue in my faith.

"[God is a unity, but] this is not a barren undifferentiated unity. God is also the fullness of being, and embraces within himself all the richness of being. Being is not to be regarded as an empty abstraction, but as a *plenum*."[1]

---

1. Macquarrie 1984, 177. I am indebted to my colleague Ted Ulrich for this reference.

Bibliography

Ackerman, Susan. 1989. *Under Every Green Tree: Popular Religion in Sixth-Century Judah*. Harvard Semitic Monographs. Edited by Frank Moore Cross. Atlanta: Scholars Press.

Adam, A. K. M., ed. 2001. *Postmodern Interpretations of the Bible*. St. Louis: Chalice Press.

Ahlstrom, G. W. 1963. *Aspects of Syncretism in Israelite Religion*. Translated by Eric J. Sharpe. Lund: G. W. K. Gleerup.

Albertz, Rainer, and Bob Becking. 2003. "Problems and Possibilities: Perspectives on Postexilic Yahwism." Pages xi–xxi in *Yahwism after the Exile: Perspectives on Israelite Religion in the Persian Era*. Edited by Rainer Albertz and Bob Becking. Assen: Van Gorcum.

Albright, W. F. 1919. "The Mouth of the Rivers." *American Journal of Semitic Languages and Literature* 35:161–95.

———. 1920. "The Goddess of Life and Wisdom." *American Journal of Semitic Languages* 36: 258–94.

———. 1957. *From the Stone Age to Christianity: Monotheism and the Historical Process*. 2nd ed. Baltimore: Johns Hopkins Press.

———. 1969. "The Moabite Stone." Page 320 in *Ancient Near Eastern Texts Relating to the Old Testament*. Edited by James B. Pritchard. Princeton, NJ: Princeton University Press.

Aletti, Jean-Noel. 1976. "Proverbes 8,22–31. 25–37 Etude de structure." *Biblica* 57:1:25–37.

Barr, James. 1993. *The Garden of Eden and the Hope of Immortality*. Minneapolis: Fortress Press.

———. 1999. *The Concept of Biblical Theology*. Minneapolis: Fortress Press.

Barrois, G. A. 1962. "Zion." Pages 879–83 in vol. 4 of *Interpreter's Dictionary of the Bible*. Edited by George Arthur Buttrick. Nashville: Abingdon Press.

Begg, Christopher. 1993. "Filling in the Blanks: Josephus' Version of the Campaign of the Three Kings: 2 Kings 3." *Hebrew Union College Annual* 64:89–110.

Bergen, Wesley J. 1992. "The Prophet Alternative: Elisha and the Israelite Monarchy." In *Elijah and Elisha in Socio-Literary Perspective*. Edited by Robert B. Coote. Atlanta: Scholars Press.

Berlinerblau, J. 1993. "The 'Popular Religion' Paradigm in Old Testament Research: A Sociological Critique." *Journal for the Study of the Old Testament* 60:3–26.

Berquist, Jon L. 1995. *Judaism in Persia's Shadow: A Social and Historical Approach*. Minneapolis: Fortress Press.

———. 2000. "Wisdom and Scribes in Persian Yehud." Paper presented at the annual meeting of the Society of Biblical Literature, Nashville, Tennessee, November 21.

———. 2003. "Critical Spatiality and the Uses of Theory." Pages 64–80 in *Imagining "Biblical Worlds": Studies in Spatial, Social, and Historical Constructs in Honour of James W. Flanagan.* Edited by David M. Gunn and Paula McNutt. London: T. & T. Clark International.

Biddle, Mark E. 1991. "The Figure of Lady Jerusalem: Identification, Deification, and Personification of Cities in the Ancient Near East." Pages 173–94 in *The Biblical Canon in Comparative Perspective.* Edited by K. L. Younger et al. Lewiston, NY: Edwin Mellen.

Bolle, Kees W. 1987. "Fate." Pages 290–98 in vol. 5 of *The Encyclopedia of Religion.* Edited by Mircea Eliade. New York: Macmillan.

Bonnard, P. 1970. "De la sagesse personifiee dans l'Ancien Testament à la sagesse en personne dans le Nouveau." Pages 117–49 in *La Sagesse de l'Ancien Testament.* Edited by M. Gilbert. Louvain: Duculot.

Brown, Francis, S. R. Driver, and Charles A. Briggs. 1978. *A Hebrew and English Lexicon of the Old Testament.* Oxford: Clarendon Press.

Burnett, Joel S. 2001. *A Reassessment of Biblical Elohim.* Atlanta: Society of Biblical Literature.

Burns, J. B. 1990. "Why Did the Besieging Army Withdraw?" *Zeitschrift für die alttestamentliche Wissenschaft* 102:187–94.

Camp, Claudia V. 1985. *Wisdom and the Feminine in the Book of Proverbs.* Sheffield: Almond Press.

———. 1987. "Woman Wisdom as Root Metaphor: A Theological Consideration." Pages 45–76 in *The Listening Heart: Essays in Wisdom and the Psalms in Honor of Roland E. Murphy.* Edited by Kenneth G. Hoglund et al. Sheffield: Sheffield Academic Press.

———. 2003. "Storied Space, or Ben Sira 'Tells' a Temple." Pages 64–80 in *Imagining "Biblical Worlds": Studies in Spatial, Social, and Historical Constructs in Honour of James W. Flanagan.* Edited by David M. Gunn and Paula McNutt T. & T. Clark International.

Campbell, Anthony F. 1975. *The Ark Narrative, 1 Sam 4–6, 2 Sam 6: A Form-Critical and Traditio-Historical Study.* Missoula, MT: Scholars Press.

Carroll, John. 1992. "The Myth of the Empty Land." *Semeia* 59:79–94.

Cazelles, Henri. 1995. "Ahiqar, *Umman* and *Amun* and Biblical Wisdom Texts." Pages 45–55 in *Solving Riddles and Untying Knots: Essays in Honor of Jonas Greenfield.* Edited by Ziony Zevit et al. Winona Lake, IN: Eisenbrauns.

Clifford, R. 1993. "Woman Wisdom in the Book of Proverbs." Pages 61–72 in *Biblische Theologie und gesellschaftlicher Wandel.* Edited by G. Braulick. Freiburg: Herder.

Collins, John J. 1997. "Jewish Monotheism and Christian Theology." Pages 81–105 in *Aspects of Monotheism: How God Is One.* Edited by Hershel Shanks. Washington, DC: Biblical Archaeological Society.

Conzelmann, H. 1971. "The Mother of Wisdom." Pages 230–43 in *The Future of Our Religious Past: Essays in Honour of Rudolf Bultmann.* Edited by James McConkey Robinson. London: SCM Press.

Crenshaw, James L. 1981. *Old Testament Wisdom: An Introduction.* Atlanta: John Knox Press.

———. 2000. "Theodicy in the Psalter." Paper presented at the Catholic Biblical Association, Los Angeles, August 6.

Curtis, Edward M. 1992. "Idol, Idolatry." Pages 376–81 in vol. 3 of *Anchor Bible Dictionary.* Edited by David Noel Freedman. New York: Doubleday.

Dahood, Mitchell. 1968. "Proverbs 8,22–31: Translation and Commentary." *Catholic Biblical Quarterly* 30:512–21.

———. 1994. *Psalms II: 51–100, A New Translation with Introduction and Commentary.* Garden City, NY: Doubleday.

Davies, G. Henton. 1962. "Worship in the Old Testament." Pages 879–83 in vol. 4 of *Interpreter's Dictionary of the Bible.* Nashville: Abingdon Press.

Davies, Philip. 1995. *Whose Bible Is It Anyway?* JSOT Supplement Series. Sheffield: Sheffield Academic Press.

Day, John. 1992. "Asherah." Pages 483–87 in vol. 1 of *Anchor Bible Dictionary.* New York: Doubleday.

———. 1998. *Wisdom in Ancient Israel: Essays in Honour of J. A. Emerton.* Edited by John Day et al. Cambridge: Cambridge University Press.

———. 2000. *Yahweh and the Gods and Goddesses of Canaan.* Sheffield: Sheffield Academic Press.

Day, Peggy Lynn. 1986. *Satan in the Hebrew Bible.* PhD dissertation. Harvard University.

Delcor, M. 1964. "Jahweh et Dagon." *Vetus Testamentum* 14:136–54.

Dever, William G. 1997. "Folk Religion in Early Israel: Did Yahweh Have a Consort?" Pages 27–56 in *Aspects of Monotheism: How God Is One.* Edited by Hershel Shanks. Washington, DC: Biblical Archaeological Society.

Donner, H. 1958. "Die religionsgeschichtlichen Ursprunge von Rov. Sal. 8." *Zeitschrift für ägyptische sprache und altertumskunde* 82:8–18.

Edelman, Diana Vikander, ed. 1995. *The Triumph of Elohim: From Yahwisms to Judaisms.* Grand Rapids: Wm. B. Eerdmans Publishing Co.

Eilberg-Schwartz, Howard. 1994. *God's Phallus and Other Problems for Men and Monotheism.* Boston: Beacon Press.

Emerton, J. A. 1960. "Some New Testament Notes: I. The Interpretation of Psalm LXXXII in John X." *Journal of Theological Studies* 11:329–32.

Flanagan, James W. "The Trialectics of Biblical Studies." http://www.cwru.edu/affil/GAIR/papers/2001papers/flanagan1.htm.

Fontaine, C. R. 1988. "The Personification of Wisdom." Pages 501–3 in *Harper's Bible Commentary.* San Francisco: Harper & Row.

Fox, Michael V. 1996. "'Amon Again." *Journal of Biblical Literature* 115:699–702.

———. 1997. "Ideas of Wisdom in Proverbs 1–9." *Journal of Biblical Literature* 116:613–33.

Frymer-Kensky, Tikva Simone. 1992. *In the Wake of the Goddesses: Women, Culture, and the Biblical Transformation of Pagan Myth.* New York: Free Press.

Gergen, Wesley J. 1992. "The Prophetic Alternative: Elisha and the Israelite Monarchy." Pages 127–38 in *Elijah and Elisha in Socioliterary Perspective.* Edited by Robert B. Coote. Atlanta: Scholars Press.

Gese, Hartmut. 1981. "Wisdom, Son of Man, and the Origins of Christology: The Consistent Development of Biblical Theology." *Horizons in Biblical Theology* 3:23–58.

Gibson, J. C. L. 1977. *Canaanite Myths and Legends.* Edinburgh: T. & T. Clark.

Gnuse, Robert Karl. 1997. *No Other Gods: Emergent Monotheism in Israel.* Sheffield: Sheffield Academic Press.

Goldingay, John. 1997. "Isaiah 40–55 in the 1990s: Among Other Things, Deconstructing, Mystifying, Intertextual, Social, Critical, and Hearer-Involving." *Biblical Interpretation* 5:225–46.

Gottwald, Norman K. 1979. *The Tribes of Yahweh.* New York: Orbis Books.

———. 1992. "Social Class and Ideology in Isaiah 40–55." *Semeia* 59:43–57.

Gray, John. 1970. *I and II Kings: A Commentary.* 2nd ed. Philadelphia: Westminster Press.

Hadley, Judith M. 1995. "Wisdom and the Goddess." Pages 234–53 in *Wisdom in Ancient Israel: Essays in Honour of J. A. Emerton*. Edited by John Day et al. Cambridge: Cambridge University Press.

Handy, Lowell K. 1990. "Sounds, Words, and Meanings in Psalm 82." *Journal for the Study of the Old Testament* 47:51–66.

Harrelson, Walter. 1969. *From Fertility Cult to Worship*. Garden City, NY: Doubleday.

———. 1970. "The Significance of Cosmology in the Ancient Near East." Pages 237–52 in *Translating and Interpreting the Old Testament*. Edited by H. T. Frank and W. L. Reed. Nashville: Abingdon Press.

Hayes, John H. and J. Maxwell Miller. 1990. *Israelite and Judean History*. Philadelphia: Trinity Press International.

Hess, Richard S. 2004. "Aspects of Israelite Personal Names and Pre-Exilic Israelite Religion." Paper presented to the International Conference of the Society of Biblical Literature, Groningen, Netherlands.

Hurtado, L. W. 1998. "First Century Jewish Monotheism." *Journal for the Study of the New Testament* 71:3–26.

Johnson, Aubrey R. 1955. *Sacral Kingship in Ancient Israel*. Cardiff: University of Wales Press.

Jones, G. H. 1984. *1 and 2 Kings*. Grand Rapids: Wm. B. Eerdmans Publishing Co.

Kaufmann, Yehezkel. 1960. *The Religion of Israel, from Its Beginning to the Babylonian Exile*. Translated and abridged by Moshe Greenberg. Chicago: University of Chicago Press.

Kautzsch, E., and A. E. Cowley. 1982. *Gesenius' Hebrew Grammar*. Oxford: Clarendon Press.

Keel, Othmar, and Christoph Uehlinger. 1992. *Gods, Goddesses, and Images of God in Ancient Israel*. Translated by Thomas H. Trapp. Minneapolis: Fortress Press.

Kelly, J. N. D. 1965. *Early Christian Doctrines*. London: A. C. Black.

Kelly, Sidney Legrand, Jr. 1968. *The Zion-Victory Songs*. PhD dissertation. Vanderbilt University.

Kloppenborg, John S. 1982. "Isis and Sophia in the Book of Wisdom." *Harvard Theological Review* 75:57–84.

Knox, W. L. 1938. "The Divine Wisdom." *Journal of Theological Studies* 38:230–37.

Kraus, Hans-Joachim. 1960. *Psalmen, 1. Teilband, Psalmen 1–59*. Neukirchen: Neukirchener Verlag.

———. 1966. *Worship in Israel*. Translated by Geoffrey Buswell. Richmond: John Knox Press.

———. 1988. *Psalms 1–59: A Commentary*. Translated by Hilton C. Oswald. Minneapolis: Augsburg Publishing House.

Kselman, John. 1990. "Psalms." Pages 523–52 in *New Jerome Biblical Commentary*. Edited by Raymond Brown. Englewood Cliffs, NJ: Prentice-Hall.

Landes, G. 1974. "Creation Tradition in Proverbs 8,22–31 and Gen 1." Pages 279–93 in *A Light unto My Path: Old Testament Studies in Honor of Jacob M. Myers*. Edited by H. N. Bream. Philadelphia: Temple University Press.

Lang, Bernhard. 1975. *Frau Weisheit*. Düsseldorf: Patmos-Verlag.

———. 1983. *Monotheism and the Prophetic Minority: An Essay in Biblical History and Sociology*. Sheffield: Almond Press.

———. 1986. *Wisdom and the Book of Proverbs: An Israelite Goddess Redefined*. New York: Pilgrim Press.

———. 1999. "Wisdom." Pages 900–905 in *Dictionary of Deities and Demons in the Bible*. Edited by Karel van der Toorn. Leiden: E. J. Brill.

Liver, J. 1967. "The Wars of Mesha, King of Moab." *Palestine Exploration Quarterly* 99:1431.

Lohfink, N. 1969. "Gott und die Götter im Alten Testament." *Theologische Akademie* 6:50–71.

Lohse, Eduard. 1971. "Sion, Jerusalem." In vol. 7 of *Theological Dictionary of the New Testament*. Edited by Gerhard Kittel and Gerhard Friedrich. Translated by Geoffrey W. Bromiley. Grand Rapids: Wm. B. Eerdmans Publishing Co.

Long, Burke O. 1991. *2 Kings*. Grand Rapids: Wm. B. Eerdmans Publishing Co.

———. 1997. "Letting Rival Gods Be Rivals: Biblical Theology in a Postmodern Age." Pages 222–33 in *Problems in Biblical Theology*. Edited by Henry T. C. Sun et al. Grand Rapids: Wm. B. Eerdmans Publishing Co.

Mack, Burton Lee. 1970. "Wisdom Myth and Mytho-logy." *Interpretation* 24:46–60.

Macquarrie, John. 1984. *In Search of Deity*. New York: Crossroad Publishing.

Maier, Christl M. 2003. "Daughter Zion as a Gendered Space in the Book of Isaiah." Paper given at the Construction of Ancient Space Seminar, AAR/SBL annual meeting, Atlanta. Available at the Web site http://www.cwru.edu/affil/GAIR/papers/2003papers/maier.pdf.

Marcus, Ralph. 1950–1951. "On Biblical Hypostases of Wisdom." *Hebrew Union College Annual*, 23:157–71.

Margalit, Baruch. 1986. "Why King Mesha of Moab Sacrificed His Oldest Son." *Biblical Archeology Review* (November–December): 62–63.

Matthews, Victor H., and Don C. Benjamin. 1991. *Old Testament Parallels: Laws and Stories from the Ancient Near East*. New York: Paulist Press.

Mayes, Andrew D. H. 1997. "*Kuntillet ʿAjrud* and the History of Israelite Religion." Pages 157ff. in *Archaelogy and Biblical Interpretation*. Edited by John R. Bartlett. London: Routledge.

McCarter, P. Kyle, Jr. 1997. "The Religious Reforms of Hezekiah and Josiah." Pages 57–80 in *Aspects of Monotheism: How God Is One*. Edited by Hershel Shanks. Washington, DC: Biblical Archaeological Society.

McKane, John. 1970. *Proverbs: A New Approach*. Old Testament Library. Philadelphia: Westminster Press.

Miller, Patrick D., Jr. 1987. "The Absence of the Goddess in Israelite Religion." *Hebrew Annual Review* 10:239–48.

———. 2000. "Israelite Religion." Pages 130–31 in *Israelite Religion and Biblical Theology: Collected Essays*. Sheffield: Sheffield Academic Press.

Miller, Patrick D., Jr., and J. J. M. Roberts. 1977. *The Hand of the Lord: A Reassessment of the "Ark Narrative" of 1 Samuel*. Baltimore: Johns Hopkins University Press.

Montgomery, James A. 1950. *A Critical and Exegetical Commentary on the Books of Kings*. Edinburgh: T. & T. Clark.

Mowinckel, Sigmund. 1962. *The Psalms in Israel's Worship*. Vol. 1. Translated by D. R. Ap-Thomas. New York: Abingdon Press.

Mullen, E. Theodore. 1980. *The Divine Council in Canaanite and Early Hebrew Literature*. Chico, CA: Scholars Press.

Murphy, Roland. 1978. "Wisdom Theses and Hypotheses." Pages 35–42 in *Israelite Wisdom: Theological and Literary Essays in Honor of Samuel Terrien*. Edited by John G. Gammie et al. Missoula, MT: Scholars Press.

———. 1988. "Wisdom and Eros in Proverbs 1–9." *Catholic Biblical Quarterly* 50:601–3.

————. 1990. *The Tree of Life: An Exploration of Biblical Wisdom Literature.* New York: Doubleday.

————. 1995. "The Personification of Wisdom." Pages 222–33 in *Wisdom in Ancient Israel: Essays in Honour of J. A. Emerton.* Edited by John Day et al. Cambridge: Cambridge University Press.

————. 1998. *Proverbs.* Word Biblical Commentary. Nashville: Thomas Nelson.

Nelson, Richard D. 1987. *First and Second Kings.* Atlanta: John Knox Press.

Newsome, Carol A. 1989. "Woman and the Discourse of Patriarchal Wisdom: A Study of Proverbs 1–9." Pages 142–60 in *Gender and Difference in Ancient Israel.* Edited by Peggy L. Day. Minneapolis: Fortress Press.

Oded, Bustenay. 1977. "Judah and the Exile." Pages 435–88 in *Israelite and Judean History.* Edited by John H. Hayes and J. Maxwell Miller. London: SCM Press.

Olyan, Saul M. 1988. *Asherah and the Cult of Yahweh in Israel.* Atlanta: Scholars Press.

Patai, Raphael. 1967a. *The Hebrew Goddess.* New York: Ktav Publishing House.

————. 1967b. *Man and Temple in Ancient Jewish Myth and Ritual.* New York: Ktav Publishing House.

Pellett, David C. 1973. "Jerusalem the Golden." *Encounter* 34:272–81.

Penchansky, David. 1989. *The Betrayal of God: Dissonance in Job.* Louisville, KY: Westminster/ John Knox Press.

————. 1997. "God the Monster: Fantasy in the Garden of Eden." Pages 43–60 in *The Monstrous and the Unspeakable: The Bible as Fantastic Literature.* Edited by George Aichele and Tina Pippin. Sheffield: Sheffield Academic Press.

————. 1999. *What Rough Beast: Images of God in the Hebrew Bible.* Louisville, KY: Westminster John Knox Press.

————. 2001. "Is Hokmah an Israelite Goddess, and What Should We Do about It?" Pages 81–92 *Post-modern Interpretations of the Bible: A Reader.* Edited by A. K. M. Adam. St. Louis: Chalice Press.

Porter, Barbara Nevling, ed. 2000. *One God or Many? Concepts of Divinity in the Ancient World.* N.p.: Casco Bay Assyriological Institute.

Pritchard, A. B. *Ancient Near Eastern Texts Relating to the Old Testament.* Princeton, NJ: Princeton University Press, 1969.

Rad, Gerhard von. 1962. *Old Testament Theology.* Vol. 1. Translated by D. M. G. Stalker. New York: Harper & Row.

————. 1972. *Wisdom in Israel.* Nashville: Abingdon Press.

Ringgren, Helmer. 1947. *Word and Wisdom: Studies in the Hypostatization of Divine Qualities and Function in the Ancient Near East.* Lund: Hakan Ohlssons Boktryckeri.

————. 1967. "The Problem of Fatalism." Pages 7–8 in *Fatalistic Beliefs in Religion, Folklore, and Literature.* Edited by Helmer Ringgren. Stockholm: Almqvist & Wiksell.

Roberts, J. J. M. 1973. "The Davidic Origin of the Zion Tradition." *Journal of Biblical Literature* 92:329–44.

————. 1976. "Zion Tradition." Pages 985–86 in *Interpreter's Dictionary of the Bible.* Supplementary Volume. Edited by Keith Crim. Nashville: Abingdon Press.

Robinson, A. 1974. "Zion and SAPHON in Psalm XLVIII 3." *Vetus Testamentum* 24:118–23.

Robinson, J. 1976. *The Second Book of Kings.* Cambridge: Cambridge University Press.

Rogers, Cleon Z. III. 1997. "The Meaning and Significance of the Hebrew Word ʾamun in Proverbs 8,30." *Zeitschrift für die alttestamentliche Wissenschaft* 109:208–21.

Rost, L. 1965. "Die Überlieferung von der Thronnachfolge Davids." Pages 119–253 in *Das Kleine Credo und andere Studien zum Alten Testament*. Heidelberg: Quelle & Meyer.

Rowley, H. H. 1967. *Worship in Israel*. London: SPCK.

Savignac, J. de. 1969. "Interpretation de Proverbes VIII 22–31." Vetus Testamentum Supplements 17:196–203.

Schicklberger, Franz. 1973. *Die Ladeerzählungen des ersten Samuel-Buches*. Würtzburg: Echter.

Schmid, Herbert. 1955. "Jahwe and die Kulttraditionen von Jerusalem." *Zeitschrift für die alttestamentliche Wissenschaft* 67:168–97.

Schmidt, Brian B. 1995. "The Aniconic Tradition: On Reading Images and Viewing Texts." Pages 75–105 in *The Triumph of Elohim*. Edited by Diana Vikander Edelman. Grand Rapids: Wm. B. Eerdmans Publishing Co.

Schwartz, Regina M. 1997. *The Curse of Cain: The Violent Legacy of Monotheism*. Chicago: University of Chicago Press.

Schweitzer, Stephen. 1999. "The 'Gods,' Children of the Most High [Psalm 58 and 82]." Presentation to the Society of Biblical Literature, St. Paul, MN, April 9.

Scott, R. B. Y. 1960. "Wisdom in Creation: The ʾamon in Prov. 8,30." *Vetus Testamentum* 10:213–23.

———. 1965. *Proverbs. Ecclesiastes*. Anchor Bible Commentary. Garden City, NY: Doubleday.

Silberman, Lou. 1985. "Metaphors of Faith." Paper presented at Vanderbilt University, Cole Lecture Series.

Smith, Mark S. 1987. *Early History of God: Yahweh and the Other Deities in Ancient Israel*. San Francisco: Harper & Row.

———. 1999. "R. K. Gnuse, No Other Gods: Emergent Monotheism in Israel." *Biblica* 80:124–27.

———. 2001. *The Origins of Biblical Monotheism: Israel's Polytheistic Background and the Ugaritic Texts*. New York: Oxford University Press.

Smith, Morton. 1971. *Palestinian Parties and Politics That Shaped the Old Testament*. New York: Columbia University Press.

Snaith, Norman H. 1954. "II Kings." Pages 187–340 in vol. 3 of *Interpreter's Bible*. New York: Abingdon Press.

Stecher, R. 1953. "Die personliche Weisheit in den Proverbien Kap 8." *Zeitschrift für Theologie und Kirche* 75:411–51.

Stern, E. 1989. "What Happened to the Cult Figurines? Israelite Religion Purified after the Exile." *Biblical Archaeology Review* 15:22–29, 53.

Stern, Philip D. 1993. "Of Kings and Moabites: History and Theology in 2 Kings 3 and the Mesha Inscription." *Hebrew Union College Annual* 64:1–14.

Stinespring, W. F. 1965. "No Daughter of Zion: A Study of the Appositional Genitive in Hebrew Grammar." *Encounter* 26:133–41.

Stolz, F. 1976. "Zion." Pages 543–51 in vol. 2 of *Theologisches Handwörterbuch zum Alten Testament*. Edited by Ernst Jenni. Munich: Chr. Kaiser Verlag.

Terrien, Samuel. 1970. "The Omphalos Myth and Hebrew Religion." *Vetus Testamentum* 20:315–38.

———. 1981. "The Play of Wisdom: Turning Point in Biblical Theology." *Horizons in Biblical Theology* 125–153.

Thompson, Thomas L. 1995. "The Intellectual Matrix of Early Biblical Narrative." Pages 107–24 in *The Triumph of Elohim*. Edited by Diana Vikander Edelman. Grand Rapids: Wm. B. Eerdmans Publishing Co.

Tigay, Jeffrey H. 1986. *You Shall Have No Other Gods: Israelite Religion in the Light of Hebrew Inscriptions*. Howard Semitic Studies 31. Atlanta: Scholars Press.

Toy, Crawford H. 1899. *A Critical and Exegetical Commentary on the Book of Proverbs*. New York: Charles Scribner's Sons.

Vawter, Bruce. 1980. "Prov. 8:22: Wisdom and Creation." *Journal of Biblical Literature* 99:205–16.

Versnel, H. S. 2000. "Three Greek Experiments in Oneness." Pages 79–163 in *One God or Many? Concepts of Divinity in the Ancient World*. Edited by Barbara Nevling Porter. N.p.: Casco Bay Assyriological Institute.

Weiser, Artur. 1962. *The Psalms: A Commentary*. Philadelphia: Westminster Press.

Whybray, R. N. 1989. *Ecclesiastes*. Grand Rapids: Wm. B. Eerdmans Publishing Co.

———. 1994. *Proverbs: The New Century Bible Commentary*. Grand Rapids: Wm. B. Eerdmans Publishing Co.

Widengren, George. 1977. "The Persian Period." Pages 458–538 in *Israelite and Judean History*. Edited by John H. Hayes and J. Maxwell Miller. Philadelphia: SCM Press.

Wright, G. Ernest. 1957. *The Old Testament against Its Environment*. London: SCM Press.

Wyatt, N. 1996. *Myths of Power: A Study of Royal Myth and Ideology in Ugaritic and Biblical Tradition*. Munich: Ugarit-Verlag.

Yee, G. 1982. "An Analysis of Prov 8:22–31 according to Style and Structure." *Zeitschrift für die alttestamentliche Wissenschaft* 94:48–66.

Yusa, Michiko. 1987. "Chance." Pages 192–96 in vol. 3 of *The Encyclopedia of Religion*. Edited by Mircea Eliade. New York: Macmillan.

Zevit, Ziony. 2001. *The Religions of Ancient Israel: A Synthesis of Parallactic Approaches*. London and New York: Continuum.

Index of Ancient Sources

Hebrew Bible

Genesis

1, 2–3, 10	29
1:2	24
1:26	29
1:27	49, 75
2	33
3:22	30
6–9	5
6:1–4	25, 34
14:18	68 n.3
16:2	15
18:2	30
18:16	31
18:21–22	31
19:21	31
22	4–5
24:12	14
26:8	56
32:6	56
38:7	14
42:29	15
44:29	16 n.12
49:25	71 n.6

Exodus

3:18	15 nn.7, 8
4:24	14
15:11	ix
20:3	ix, 33, 43–44
32:10	5

Numbers

11:12	57 n.14
23:3, 4, 15, 16	15 nn.7, 8

Deuteronomy

2:9	8 n.10
4:19	37 n.9
6:4	x
13:13	71 n.6
20:19	8
23:11 (Eng. 23:10)	16
25:17–18	15 n.7, 16
32:8–9	ix–x, 34, 36 n.4, 77 n.1, 93
33:13	71

Joshua

10:1, 3	68 n.3

Judges

3:7	75 n.1
11	4
11:24	8

Ruth

2:3	16 nn.10, 11; 17, 18 n.17
4:16	57

1 Samuel

1:6	16 n.11
6:9	13, 17, 18 n.17
20:26	16, 18 n.17
24	67
28:10	16 n.12

2 Samuel

12:16	15

1 Kings

1	16
14:15	77 n.3
14:23	77 n.3
15:13	75 n.1, 76
16:32	77 n.3
17	7, 11
18	76 n.2
18:3–4	77
18:19	75
22	28, 34

2 Kings

2:23–25	14
12:2	9

101

Index of Subjects